I Want To Be Just Like You…

"NO YOU DON'T"

By: *Carolyn White-Mosley*

Due to the nature of the content, parental discretion is advised.

Published by: Carolyn's Love

Editors: Latasha (FabralaJor) & Rose Smith

Sketch Artist: Ayrel White

Paint Design Artist: Lynda Coleman

Email: carolynslovesbooks@gmail.com

Website: http://carolynslove.webs.com/

ISBN: 978-0-9916270-0-4

Copyright: 2014

I Want To Be Just Like You   "No You Don't"

Carolyn White- Mosley
Carolyn's Love

All rights reserved. No part of this publication may be reproduced, stored in a retrieval system, or transmitted in any form by   any means electronic, mechanical, photocopy, recording, or otherwise. Carolyn White-Mosley owns all rights to her story, and publication.

Important Publisher's Note:

The names in this story are the reflection of you and many others. The author, Carolyn White- Mosley, also takes complete and ALL legal responsibility. The publisher is legally free of any and ALL claims of responsibility regarding the content written about herein.

Purpose

This book is written as a guide to the misguided individual, seeking solutions for their unanswered questions. Uniquely compiled of "Lessons Learned", many may find that reading each chapter will provide them a clear understanding of how the definition of 'Love' is often tainted by generational ignorance.

Cmo, the name of the main character, is an individual victimized by abuse. Her story is written to shed light on the issues that arise daily, with both men and women. Her life is documented to reflect a lack of compassion and a deficiency in the skill of parenting, and how these two subjects combined can have a major influence on the way a person survives. No, parenting does not come with a manual because we [as parents] are not perfect. However, covering up our mistakes or not acknowledging our wrongs in the presence of our children can cause confusion and distrust. "Do as I say, not as I do" is a phrase often spoken by parents, but we fail to understand that our children mimic our actions. Allow your child to see you make mistakes, but also show them how to correct it. Cmo means "see more". You may see yourself in Cmo, and if so, don't allow your actions to continue on, seek help. We, as parents, are not alone; there are individuals suffering from the same mental abuse, social abuse, and physical abuse as Cmo and her family; but never faced the issues head on. Cmo lived the pain and decided 'enough is enough'; and so can you.

To that end, the Author's main purpose consists of clarifying the concept "LOVE" to each individual reader. "Learning Our Value Everyday" revisits the idea of self – appreciation. Embrace your flaws, they're the prefect little imperfects that make you unique in all of your ways. Stop trying to be like others, because you don't know the struggles they've gone through; know your worth. The Author's message to all is: "I Thank God for Who I am, Yes I do." Take the negative words, negative vibes, negative thinking, and negative emotions away from the equation, and replace them with positive reinforcements. Begin to walk in peace, love, and confidence, only then would you have learned the progression of self-improvement. 'Self' is the focus of life; life is the focus of love.

LOVE: "Learning Our Value Every Day."

UNDERSTAND: Self-love.

LEARNING: Appreciation, Forgiveness, Compassion.

Dedications

Virgil Lee White and Carolyn S. Hutchinson-White

Thank you for being the best parents for me in this day and time. Teaching me the skills needed for parenting. I am learning the meaning of "LOVE" as a daily bread. Thank you for the foundation of love and feeding me the appreciation of God.

Cassma L. Taylor-Ford

Thank you for being patient with me baby; I love you! As a parent, I have made a multitude of mistakes in rearing you and for this, I ask you to forgive me. I would like to begin anew relationship for our future. You're the one who helped me to realize how a mother should treat her children. Your compassion and love is amazing to your babies. I am proud of you and the mother you have become. I appreciate the mother in you! Keep on showing me how to become the mother you desire.

Deceased

Daughter Ortralla L. Mosley and Son Taylor

I thank you both for the love I received from you and that love is the love that I will carry on as my guide to better myself.

Grandbabies

Isaiah Jordan, Dezire Tizeno and Symon Tizeno

Thank you for helping me to become a grandmother with unconditional love; love that motivates me to be the grandmother I have always wanted to be. I love you all!

First lady Judith L. Walker and Pastor Amalaneze L. Heron

There was a time I did not want to understand the Church. I have missed out on plenty of joyous occasions because of my stubbornness. I now know that prayer has been your guide. I thank God for your prayers geared towards me, protecting me, in my growth. I have wronged you both, many times, and for that I ask for forgiveness. This book has taught me how to consider me and my evil doings and for that I am grateful for the insight. Prayer does cover a multitude of faults. I love you both!

Virgil L. White Jr.

With you I am short with words as you are. Jr. the love that we share is appreciated above all. You are a great example to me as a man and a brother. I love you man!!!

Marry Russaw

Thank you for ALL of the lessons learned. Your encouraging and inspirational words helped me to move forward with life.

Christine Harris

Thank you for the insight and push to do better. You never gave up on me. I love you!

In Appreciations of My Spiritual Foundation

Thank you God; for your love; for your compassion; your patients, your peace, the vision, and preparing me for my assignments ahead. Thank you God for lessons learned.

Pastor Anthony Walker, Open Door COGIC, Austin TX

Pastor Michel Heron, Purpose Church of Denton, Denton, TX

Dexter and Linda Lewis, Agape COGIC, Dallas, TX

Elder Edward and Sister Jaquilin Calloway, Lighthouse COGIC, Dallas, TX

Barbara Calloway, Barbara Callaway Ministries, Dallas, TX

Elder Ron Burch & First Lady Audrey Burch, New Life Church of God in Christ, Lancaster, TX

Special Thanks

Erica Carroll and Family

Thank you for being the friend that stood by me, gave me spiritual advice, corrected me when needed, helped me with homework assignments, reminded me that greater is coming and never to give up; constantly telling me I can make it with God on my side and through all my issues, pains, disappointments I will prevail in Jesus name. I love you.

Lynda Coleman

Lynda Coleman is a gifted artist that has been painting since the age of 5. She has been exhibiting her artwork throughout the City of Austin, Texas since 1988. Hundreds of youth have been instructed and inspired by Lynda Coleman's Art From The Heart workshops. Lynda is not only a Visual Artist, but she is also a poetess, who has self-published two poetry books. Through her art and poetry she shares her love of God; as her works express love, joy, peace and healing to hurting souls.

Rose Smith

Rose Smith is an editor, self-published author of four books, Life Coach, Creator of ROSEISMS, Founder of R.O.S.E.S (Reaching Out Supporting Every Sister) Organization and the Founder of

ROSES Magazine. She loves to serve God and His people, and her passion is to help promote personal growth in women and their families. She truly believes that everyone's journey matters. And, she encourages people to maximize their potential while she strives to do the same. Her motto is "Leading by example is life's best teacher." ~ROSEISMS

Emotionally, I thank you for helping me to present these words to the World. I have many books of words, but only one word to describe my love towards you. You are "GREATLY" appreciated.

Thank You

To those who have crossed my path in 50+1 years of life. I thank you all for lessons learned.

Table of Contents

Chapter 1: 16-20……………………...Augustine and Douglas

Chapter 2: 22-28…………………….Augustine Leaves Home

Chapter 3: 30-40………………………….The Birth of Cmo

Chapter 4: 46-47…………………………..Cmo's Beatings

Chapter 5: 48-60………………………...Cmo's First Love

Chapter 6: 62-63……………………...Cmo Meets William

Chapter 7: 64-87…………………………William's Abuse

Chapter 8: 88-90……………………………William's Son

Chapter 9: 92-119………………….Birth of the First Child

Chapter 10: 120-125………….Cmo Goes Back To William

Chapter 11: 126-136……………………….Cmo and Steve

Chapter 12: 138-150…………….Cmo and Steve's Divorce

Chapter 13: 152-155………...Cmo Gets Her Children Back

Chapter 14: 156-165……………….Cmo Becomes Abusive

Chapter 15: 166-182……………………Patients and Peace

Chapter 16: 184-209…………………………..A Night Out

Chapter 17: 210-211……………………God-given Name

Chapter 18: 212-224…………………..Cmo Finds Herself

Chapter 19: 226-233……Cmo Finds Her Biological Father

Chapter 20: 234-237……………………..Augustine's Love

Chapter 21: 238-240……….."LOVE" Learning Our Value Everyday

INTRODUCTION

Constantly uttered into my ear, one should feel honored whenever such a statement is spoken; however when I hear these seven words my heart begins to ache. Are we in complete understanding of what *"I want to be just like you"* really means or what we may or may not request of our lives? Today, those dreadful words found its way back into my world, staining my heart once again. Though the approach was different, the effect remained the same. It caused me to reflect on my present situation and how this moment came to be. I began to muse over the story that Augustine told me many years ago.

Chapter 1

Augustine and Douglas

Growing up abused, ridiculed and neglected, Augustine was deprived of her childhood and forced to fill the role of Mother to her younger siblings at the tender age of nine. While her mother would stay out engaging in all-night drinking sessions, Augustine would constantly worry about the whereabouts of their next meal. Being the eldest, it was her responsibility to look after the household, so she would get blamed for everything that went wrong.

There was one occasion where Augustine mother's rage could be seen as physical scars. One morning, after another night of chasing the bottle, Augustine's mother entered her room with an extension cord in hand. As she, her brothers, and her sisters lie peacefully sleeping, Augustine's mother began beating her as if in a drunken fit. But no, it wasn't a bad dream or the repercussions of intoxication; the cause of this beating was due to the liquor stained glasses left in the sink and the table not being wiped clean from her mother's guest the night before. Apparently, after a day filled with cooking for, cleaning after, and grooming her siblings, Augustine was also responsible for cleaning up after her mother and her mother's male friends. She was the victim of child abuse by the hands of her mother. For so long she had associated love with pain, that is, until she met Douglas.

Augustine met Douglas while attending school, she was 14 and he was 17, but regardless of age, Augustine knew that he was someone special. She began sharing parts of herself with Douglas that she never shared with anyone before. Parts of her that awakened feelings that were beyond her years, and it seemed so wrongfully right. Not knowing, and never being taught, that strong sexual urges should not be acted upon unless protected; Augustine and Douglas's relationship continued to flourish. The non-existing bond between her and her mother prevented her from learning how to love-self. Not only a love between mother and child but, also, between man and woman.

She could only recall her mother saying, "If you ever get pregnant I will kill you." The words that ought to have come out of her mother's mouth should have been "While having sexual intercourse you will need protection; if you're not protected, there is a great possibility you may become pregnant." But unaware of the circumstances, Augustine continued to have these special moments with Douglas, and became pregnant. When Augustine found out she was pregnant she immediately said…

AUGUSTINE: "Oh my goodness, my mother is going to kill me".

Now terrified, Augustine began panicking because she knew her mother would follow through with her threats. There wasn't any other choice but to face reality and suffer the consequences, consequences that could lead to detrimental repercussions. Augustine contemplated running away from home and she began to think, *but where would I go, how will I take care of my baby, how could I support it by myself, I have nothing?* All of those thoughts ran through her mind but then she looked up to see Douglas saying something to her.

AUGUSTINE: "What did you say?"

DOUGLAS: "You can come and stay here, with us… with me."

Douglas knew his mother wouldn't mind because she constantly worked and was almost never home. And though Douglas lived with his mother and two older brothers, they were seldom there. So, Douglas ran the house with little supervision.

Although Augustine was susceptible to the living arrangement, she couldn't help but worry about the safety of her brothers and sisters. She feared that her mother would now take her anger out on her siblings because she wouldn't be around to take the abuse for them. But then again, her mother never treated her brothers and sisters the way she treated her.

Augustine was her mother's personal punching bag, she was the victim of her frustrations, but with Augustine gone who would be her mother's next target. She contemplated rethinking her decision, but then she felt little flutters in her stomach. No, it wasn't her nerves giving her butterflies, it was her baby moving around and snapping her back to reality. Augustine only had two choices, leave and be safe, or stay and live in constant fear.

So, despite the unknown, she chose to leave so that her baby would have a chance at life…a better life. Now, instead of partying all night with random men, her mother would have to cook for, clean after, and groom her own children, and at that thought, Augustine smiled.

Chapter 2

Augustine Leaves Home

Augustine moved in with Douglas, and began her new life. Leaving her mother's house was one of the hardest decisions young Augustine ever made, but she knew in her heart that is was right. Augustine was a little afraid of what Douglas's mother would say once she knew that Augustine was pregnant and living in her house, but to her surprise, Douglas's mother was accepting of the situation.

Douglas's mother told her that she had always wanted a daughter, so having Augustine around was like a gift to her from her son. Everyone got along with each other, but moving in with Douglas had its stipulations. Even though Douglas's mother was never much of a church going woman, she knew what kind of life she wanted her son to have.

A parent always wants what's best for their child.

They desire to have their child live a far better life than theirs. Douglas's mother told Douglas to do the right thing and marry Augustine, because shacking up was not the desire that she, nor God, had for their lives. Douglas's mother knew, all too well, how it felt to be a single [unwed] mother and she didn't want that for Augustine. So, Augustine and Douglas got married and christened their marriage with the birth of their bouncing baby girl; they named her Gloria.

Augustine and Douglas were excited to be first time parents, Douglas had a job bringing home a steady pay check and everything seemed to be falling into place. The young couple yearned to have a place that they could call their own. They knew that Douglas's mother loved having them their but they were still under her roof, so they had to live by her rules. Nevertheless, they made the decision to move out on their own, and with that, the happy couple found a beautiful little quaint house just big enough to raise their family. The move bought Augustine and Douglas closer, but they quickly learned that being on your own was hard.

With both of them being from shattered homes, they were deprived of the knowledge on the toils of responsibility. Neither was reared in a positive growth environment; both parenting styles displayed some form of negligence whether emotionally, physically, mentally or socially. They both lacked the proper education on how to build a positive, long lasting, relationship. They made it work the best way they knew how, with the little understanding that they did possess.

***

Augustine would often go by her mother's house to check on her siblings, mostly when her mom wasn't home. However, sometimes she would be there but there wouldn't be any conversing between the two. Secretly, Augustine would always have her mother's hurtful words running through her mind, *you ain't nothing but trash, you are never going to amount up to nothing, and you are stupid, nobody want your fat ass.* These negative thoughts were actually haunting memories of her past, when she lived with her mother. Unbeknownst to her, this was a never-ending cycle, destined to repeat itself.

***

Augustine wanted to get a job to have some extra income coming in, but then she found out that she was pregnant again, so working was definitely out of the question. She knew that things would get a little tighter, but just the thought of having another baby frightened her. With tears seeping over the brim of her eyes, she asked Douglas...

AUGUSTINE: "What are we going to do?"

DOUGLAS: "We will be alright... I'll just get a second job, and we will have to move back in with my mom".

Augustine began to cry even harder, she didn't want to move, she loved their house…she loved having her own.

AUGUSTINE: "How could this happen. This time we used a condom I don't understand, I just don't understand. You did use a condom right?"

Douglas began acting awkwardly; he saw her looking at him so he looked away from her and said,

DOUGLAS: "I didn't use one every time remember, I don't like the way they feel. I like it better without one".

Augustine was so upset by Douglas's answer that she began furiously screaming at him.

AUGUSTINE: "I told you to use one now look at what happened!"

Augustine's anger was so strong, that she couldn't even think clearly. She needed space, she needed to get away before she did something crazy; so she walked into her room and slammed the door as hard as she could behind her. She was so upset that she began trembling, Douglas walked into the room to comfort her, but she didn't want him anywhere near her. Eventually she calmed down enough for Douglas to reassure her that everything was going to be alright, but she wasn't completely comfortable about the situation. Augustine couldn't help but wonder how having a second child would affect their lives.

***

Nine months after having Gloria, a second child was born, Patrice.

Just imagine, two children in pampers, one new born and one nine months old. One breast fed and the other bottle fed, coming from a place of raising children since you were old enough to remember, to staying at home and raising your own. You're doing the same thing that you were doing in the abusive home minus the physical and mental abuse. You're staying at home day, after day, just you and the babies. No entertainment, no money, using tee shirts for diapers, lights and hot water getting shut off, bathing the children in cold water listening to their screams, husband coming home from working two jobs and all you have in the kitchen is the kitchen special (rice and beans).

To make matters worse, an eviction notice had been placed on their door.

Augustine always wanted to leave her mother's house thinking life would be differently; however she [quickly] found herself in pretty much of the same predicament for the first two and a half years of their marriage. But after a while, things began to manifest for the better.

30

Chapter 3

The Birth of Cmo

Douglas accepted an offer for a job in Cameron, Pennsylvania; this position provided him with more money, benefits, and better hours. The paychecks that Douglas had begun to bring in were enough to upgrade the family into a two bedroom apartment. They now had insurance, a 401K, and a checking's and saving's account. Life was good, and Augustine began wondering how much more of a great life it would be if she were to get a job. No sooner had she pondered that thought when, out of the blue, she received a call from her sister with some troubling news.

Her sister, all of 14 years old, was pregnant. Augustine and her mother didn't want her sister, Pamela, to have the child. Although Augustine became pregnant at the same age, her sister's situation was completely different. It would be embarrassing for all involved if anyone found out who the father of her baby was. They had to keep the secret amongst themselves. So, Augustine tried all types of home abortions on her sister like, inserting a fresh sprig of parsley and a tablet of vitamin C as far as possible into the vagina, making her drink vinegar and take laxatives, tripping her and having her fall on her belly, and even leaning her over a chair causing pressure on her belly, nothing seemed to work. Nine months later was the birth of Augustine's sister's child; they named her Cmo (yes, Cmo).

***

Cmo was given to Augustine for her to care for because Pamela was too young and Douglas felt like they should help her due to the fact that Child Protective Services were going to take the child. Augustine, however, did not want to be responsible for his child, she didn't care who got her, just as long as it wasn't her.

Cmo was a very ugly child, so ugly that Augustine would hide her in the top drawer and tell anyone who came to visit, that Cmo was asleep. As often as they had guest over, Augustine would do this just so she didn't have to show Cmo. Douglas would come home from work and hear of his wife's heinous acts towards Cmo from Cmo's older sisters. He would always question Augustine about the situations and Augustine would shrug it off like it was nothing major.

AUGUSTINE: "She's an ugly little retarded child; I get tired of her crying all the time so that's how I punish her, besides, you're the one that wanted her not me".

Augustine stated one day after Douglas found out that she had tied Cmo to a chair. Douglas advanced towards Augustine, with anger on his lips saying…

DOUGLAS: "Maybe if you wouldn't have tried all those messed up remedies to get rid of her she just may not have been born that way".

Douglas was fed up with Augustine's meaningless excuses, Augustine was hurting this innocent child but her hatred blinded the abuse.

AUGUSTINE: "Oh right..., so now it's my fault she's a retard."

Augustine folded her arms, sat on the couch and looked up at Douglas while he stood in front of her breathing rapidly.

DOUGLAS: "YOU THINK ABOUT IT!"

Augustine jumped to her feet and stormed off to her room,

AUGUSTINE: "SCREW YOU ASSHOLE!"

Meanwhile, the argument between her parents scared her, so Cmo sat on the floor and cried by her mother's door. Augustine heard Cmo's faint cries and yelled to Douglas AUGUSTINE: "Get that damn retard away from my door. You should be the one taking care of the little retard anyway; this is some messed up shit."

Douglas gently picked up Cmo and held her close to his heart and he whispered to her, DOUGLAS: "I love you; you are the light of my life, my precious love".

After about five minutes of safely resting in her father's arms, Cmo calmed down and fell fast asleep.

***

Douglas grew tired of coming home, only to be greeted by Cmo's cries, the frustration that his wife felt for taking care of their daughter was beginning to sever the strings of their marriage. He couldn't deal with the pressure, so Douglas became a workaholic and alcoholic. His job became a home away from home, and booze was his mistress. Douglas found that his peace was at work because he would be away from Augustine.

With Douglas constantly working, Augustine became a very bitter person, ferociously violent and malicious. She began to form into her mother. She became mentally, emotionally, and socially abusive to everyone. Cmo took the brunt of Augustine's wrath because she blamed her for all of her troubles. Cmo was the unwanted child she was very sick and underweight as a baby and because of her mother's abuse she was also very unhappy.

At three months old her mother would try to feed her but Cmo would reject it and this infuriated Augustine. Augustine would force feed Cmo by slapping her little fragile legs. The slap was a thunder of pain for the child. The pain would cause her to let out a loud yell and when that happened, Augustine would force table spoons of food down her little throat.

Cmo would choke, gag, or heave and sometimes regurgitate her food; which only made Augustine even more violent and she would began verbally abusing Cmo.

At the age of ten months, Cmo weighed eleven pounds 3 ounces with short black hair (nearly bald), brown eyes, and very dark skin that appeared ashy. That stage of Cmo's life became very painful as well because she still had problems with eating. Augustine's physical abuse escalated from a whaling slap on the legs, to a slap on the face. The procedure for making Cmo eat had progressed to squeezing Cmo's cheeks together, like the form of a fish's mouth, and shoving spoonsful of food into Cmo's mouth. Then Cmo's mother would pinch her lips together with her fingers holding them as tight as she could. This left bruises on Cmo's lips and around her mouth; most of the time that action would cause her to vomit. Vomit

Would come through her little nose and Augustine would let go of her malicious hold and continue to verbally abuse Cmo. Then she;d pick up the food and start to feed Cmo; vomit and all.

Cmo was, also born with Metatarsus Adductus (a curve in her foot), because of that Cmo didn't walk until she was about four years old. This was another issue that caused Augustine to hate her child. With Douglas constantly at work and never home, Cmo was raised in a house full of pain and despair. Augustine would often tell Cmo how much she hated herbecause she was retarded and ugly. Cmo had a terrible childhood, and because of this, she hardly ever smiled…happiness was foreign.

To identify and describe the most significant influence in a child's development it starts by saying that the parent's background is the initial effect. This is based upon the nurturing and the type of cultural environment the child is brought up in. The maturation and the socialization skills can/will determine his/her peer influence. The inherited characteristics of the development of a child can/will be unique. For instance, intelligence is a hereditary genetic influence that is mainly responsible for constancy in cognitive operations which increases with age; however, the families shared environment can/will have a great environmental influence on a child. A child will eventually find their own niche in life by vigorously selecting surroundings, situations, atmospheres and circumstances compatible with their hereditary abilities and connected interest.

***

When Cmo was old enough to understand, Augustine told Cmo that she was a very sickly child. Augustine admitted to Cmo that she knew she abused her, but didn't know how to stop because this was the type of lifestyle she was accustomed to. Even though Augustine saw the effects that her abuse had on Cmo, but it was too late, the damage was already done. But despite all of the information of being abused, Cmo loved Augustine very much. She loved her because Augustine was the only mother she knew, but she continued to mistreat Cmo, even after the acknowledgment of abuse.

Cmo didn't truly understand why her mother would hurt her like she had. She didn't know how to make her mother love or accept her, so Cmo would act out in ways of rebellion. Cmo would lie and be disobedient so that she may obtain positive attention from Augustine. She hoped this type of behavior, in return, would receive some sort of motherly affection; unfortunately, it didn't.

Yes, Cmo was mean and rebellious, but she felt like she had to do those things because she knew her mother was incapable of helping her in a loving manner. Cmo felt as though she could never trust her mother because her mother failed to give her a sense of security. The question remained a nightmare in her head *how can you trust someone when they've told you that they had hatred towards you, tried to get rid of you, and admitted they abused you?* Cmo compared her life to dodge ball because of how often she had to dodge a slap, shoe, plate, umbrella, book, phone, picture frame, spoon, or just whatever her mother could grab a hold of first. "Why should/would a person try to do well and develop positively when their mother doesn't seem to want them to prosper in life?" that's the rhetorical question Cmo would often ask herself.

She wanted to give up and allow life to take her where it will. However, after learning of the abuse her mother endured by her mother (Cmo's grandmother) she began to see the full picture. Cmo started monitoring her mother in ways of what [not] to do if she ever had children. Cmo made a promise to herself to never become a replica of her mother.

CMO: "I will love my children unconditionally and listen to them always."

Cmo realized that just because Augustine was abusive towards her didn't condone or excuse her actions, but it did explain them. Augustine suffered from ignorance, she didn't know any better. The home training that Augustine was accustomed to consisted of abuse and neglect. She didn't have that positive support or buoyant upbringing. That discouraging pattern was the source of her family's development.

This type of family occurrence became a plague that struck the whole household, jumping from generation to generation. There are so many ways of being abused and so many ways of abusing. It's not just physical abuse but also emotional and social neglect. The emotional and social effect was the ducking and dodging of life's hurts and pains never to stand and fight for what is morally right. Only knowing that pain is life; just deal with it, keeping family, friends, associates and her community at bay from living a life of lies. Lies! Lies had caused her to experience a rollercoaster of depression, anxiety, mistrust, abuse, fear, oppression and self-depreciation. Her mother should have never hurt her in that way, shape, form, or fashion.

That's why Cmo's young life transitioned in the way that it did. She hated herself for doing what she did to herself and others. No, it wasn't a positive outlook nor was it acceptable; nevertheless, this is what Cmo felt she had to do to gain the love of her mother.

***

After learning of her mother's past, Cmo realized that her mother really loved her but in a very strange way.

The type of love that her mother exhibited was the same as her mother's before her. To strike was her way of showing love. Cmo began to tell herself ...

CMO: "She loved me the best way that she knew how to love. It's just that her way of loving me hurts." Though she grew to know and understand this, the damage had already been done and she realized that some of the things Augustine did to her had a, long lasting, scarring effect.

But, Cmo recognized that her mother was a loving person to others. Augustine never treated her other two daughters the same as Cmo. That type of unfair treating, also, had a negative effect on her relationship with her sisters. Because of this, Cmo's prayers would always be *love and have love return* but she failed to learn how to love because of her rearing.

When you are not taught the proper way to love, you can send and receive mixed signals to what you may consider to be the depiction of love. You will reject those emotions for fear of being rejected yourself. When you give good, positive love, it may also be rejected from fear of being hurt. Sometimes the, quote unquote, love that is given can scar an individual for life; especially in this case. Cmo received many whooping's because of her rebellious ways.

She understood that she needed to be disciplined at times, most children do; but Cmo's whooping's would be the consequence of minor actions. She would get abused for not washing dishes correctly, not cleaning the tile with the old tooth brush, making a B when she could have made an A, simple things that should have been resolved with words.

Granted, she understood that stealing money out of her father's drawer or lying like a sailor were punishable offenses, but failing to fold clothes correctly was not a part of that category.

Besides, her lying resulted from the fear of telling the truth because she knew her mother would hurt her. Not telling her mother everything and lying to make it sound a lot better was a way for Cmo to, hopefully, escape some of her mother's abusive routine. Augustine had a saying, "Even if you didn't do it, this is for the time you got away with it all, it all evens out." and Cmo would say in her heart, *No, no it don't even out.*

Chapter 4

Cmo's Beatings

Cmo would run as much as she could while the beatings were taking place; she felt this would tire her mom out but, actually, it was fuel for her anger. Despite the known, she ran anyway because it felt like she was saving herself from at least one cut or bruise. Cmo knew neither of her beatings panned out, not the way Augustine would beat her. Cmo felt as though, beatings and abusing were one in the same.

Augustine beat, whipped, and gave whooping's with extension cords, shoes, switches, big heavy spoons, books and whatever else she could get her hands on. For example, Cmo would have to pick three switches from the tree because in the midst of her beating, they would break.

It seemed as if she (Augustine) would never get tired of beating Cmo. Cmo's mother would beat her for so long that she would run under beds or run into a closet trying to get out of reach, pulling clothes on top of her and whatever else that would lighten the pressure of the object. If Cmo managed covering herself, Augustine would sometimes get her fist and hit her or she'd punch and kick her with such force…like it felt good to her.

Cmo remembers her eldest sister saying…

GLORIA: "Mama, don't whip her no more please"

As she and Patrice cried watching their mother whale on Cmo. Cmo said that her mom would tell her, all the time,

AUGUSTINE: "I do you like this because you remind me so much of myself. You are just me all over again and I don't want you to go through what have been through". Although Cmo was often told this in the midst of her beatings, she never understood it.

Chapter 5

Cmo's First Love

Cmo started high school and met a teacher who began to teach her home economics. This teacher is who Cmo would refer to as Miss Inspiration. Miss. Inspiration taught Cmo a different method of cooking and cleaning, and her way of teaching was gentle. Cmo would love to go to school rather than be at home because while at home she knew that the least little thing would most likely set her mother off.

Cmo would share private conversations with Miss Inspiration, often talking about her feelings and plans for the future. She would sometimes pretend that Miss Inspiration was her mother because she knew that she and Augustine would never have these kinds of discussions. Even though Cmo was an abused child, she found ways to channel her anger so that it would not interfere with the life style(s) she hoped to have one day. Cmo graduated with A's on the honor roll and she had plans for college.

Miss Inspiration was Cmo's greatest supporter; this lady would take time out to assist in all areas that were needed for Cmo to succeed in life. She was the positive adult role model to Cmo. Cmo's appearance began to change, and she started developing hips and breast. Although her clothes were not the nicest, Cmo filled them out pretty well and people started to take notice of her, especially boys.

***

Cmo began seeing a young man named Eugene in high school. She never told her mother, but Miss Inspiration knew. Cmo was afraid to tell her mother because her mother didn't trust her. Augustine would say things like "I know your fast ass out there with them boys!" But, Cmo was not fast or promiscuous in that way, yet Augustine kept her bound. So when an opportunity opened, Cmo jumped on it.

There wasn't anything Cmo wouldn't try and Augustine knew it. Augustine felt that the beatings would be her way of sparing Cmo from the pain of the world. Instead she just made her daughter want to try everything she could. This is why Cmo had been labeled as a rebellious child. She was an active child coming out of captivity. Nevertheless, while at home Cmo was restricted from boys (in her opinion "restricted from FUN"). But at school, Cmo had the freedom to do whatever she wanted, and what she wanted was a relationship with Eugene.

Eugene and Cmo was a couple from tenth grade until a little over 4 months after they graduated. When Cmo was about to turn 18, a month before her birthday, she received a beating for throwing a large spoon away. Although she had been throwing cups, plates, bowls, and utensils away for months, she had finally gotten caught. Augustine was a talker when she'd whoop Cmo, she would say things like…

AUGUSTINE: "How that feel huh, I'll kill you girl, after I'm done beating yo ass you'll think twice about it the next time, don't you do it no-more."

Each Hit would be in sync with each word, like the perfect harmonious melody. The swishing sound that the extension card made as it left her body and returned only to cut her skin in a different place seemed like music to Augustine ears. After the beating Augustine made Cmo go to the bathroom to bathe. While in the bathroom, Augustine prepared a very hot and stinging surprise for Cmo, with water so hot that her body, as dark as it was, turned red.

As Cmo sat in the scolding hot water, trying not to move because the water was burning her scars, Augustine stood in the doorway spewing hurtful insults.

AUGUSTINE: "Your black ass won't do that no more, what the hell you crying for? SHUT UP!"

Augustine said, as she leaned against the door post with her arms folded.

CMO: "But it hurts"

AUGUSTINE: "Next time remember this ass whooping. You might save yourself, now shut up before I come whoop your ass again."

Cmo sat in the tub wrenching in agony, the water was so hot that she felt her body going numb. Augustine saw that Cmo wasn't washing so she disappeared into her bedroom and Cmo could hear her mumbling to herself while she rummaged through her things. In an instant, Augustine came back into the bathroom with the stinger, a nice big bottle of rubbing alcohol. Sarcastically, Augustine said…

AUGUSTINE: "Let me make it better, we don't want those to get infected"

Then Augustine began pouring the contents of the bottle upon Cmo's head as she sat in the scolding hot water. Cmo let out a loud scream, and as tears fell over her bruised cheeks, Augustine drew back her fist and gave Cmo a big whop across her face.

AUGUSTINE: "Stand up and bend over so that I can pour this on you back."

Augustine said as she grabbed Cmo's arm trying to pull her up. Cmo stood up, shaking in terror and agony,

CMO: "I'm sorry, I won't do it again"

AUGUSTINE: "I know I'm going to make you remember."

Augustine said while pouring the alcohol on the newly made cuts and bruises.

***

Cmo starred into her mirror looking at her unrecognized reflection. On her body she had old cuts and bruises mixed with swollen new cuts and bruises, a blackened eye and a knot on the side her head as large as a lemon. She couldn't let Eugene see her like this, so she called him and told him what happened. He was furious to know that this had happened to the person he loved. But, he also became afraid for Cmo's life. Cmo told him not to tell anyone because she didn't want her mother to get in any trouble. She knew Eugene loved her and wanted to see her safe so she reassured him that she was planning to leave as soon as she turned 18 years old.

She and Eugene began making plans to have sex because she wanted him to be her first. Eugene was so protective of her that he made her feel safe and secure. This type of love felt good to Cmo and it was a love that she had never been introduced to. They would often speak of marriage and one day having a family. She wanted to run away with Eugene, he gave her the love she knew existed but never experienced.

***

Two weeks after her eighteenth birthday while her family was out shopping, she was on punishment for the spoon crimes for a month so she couldn't go anywhere, Cmo called up Eugene to see what he was doing. He wasn't doing much of anything, so she told him to come over to her house to sit and talk for a while. Eugene came over and he and Cmo decided to cuddle up and watch a little T.V.

Sitting on her mother's couch, Cmo leaned over and kissed Eugene, first with a peck on the lips, then with a deep passionate kiss. Eugene wrapped his arms around her and began to hold her with a soft compassionate embrace, rubbing his soft lips against hers. Cmo began to feel tingly all over as Eugene pressed his lips nice and snug against hers. Then suddenly, Eugene opened his mouth slightly, his warm tongue came out, softly licking the top of Cmo's lips. She followed his style and slightly opened her mouth and licked his top lip and when she tried it again he met her with his slightly open mouth and began to suck on her tongue. His smooth hands started caressing her body, going into places where only she had explored. By now, it felt like her body was on fire, never had she felt like this before. The only thing she kept thinking about was how good Eugene would feel inside of her, she had to know. They united as one and Cmo was in a land filled with an abundance of love.

This became an act of sharing their bodies, hearts, minds and souls with one another. Most would have called this a sexual encounter but to these two love mates, it was a symphony of emotions. This was unfamiliar ground for the both of them but especially for Cmo. Eugene made her feel loved and wanted, this sensation was something she yearned for all of her life. She couldn't hold back the bitter-sweet tears, so she laid her head on Eugene's shoulder and cried. Feeling the tears falling down his bare chest, Eugene looked down and asked her why she was crying, and through her sobs she managed to say…

CMO: "I never felt this way before."

Cmo was eighteen years old when she gave herself to Eugene, he was her first and she was happy that she chose him because he was gentle and he loved her very much. As Cmo and Eugene laid there, holding each other and they talked for at least an hour. For the fear of her mother coming home, Cmo jumped up and told Eugene to get dressed while she scrambled to put back on her clothes. Afterwards, she told him to leave before her parents came home to find him there.

She walked him to the door, but before he opened it, he turned and kissed her one last time and hugged her. The embrace was compassionate, it was different from any other time and they both knew that, so looking passionately into each other's eyes they said "I love you".

Cmo quickly closed the door and ran to the window to see him walking backwards looking her way throwing air kisses and she returned them to him holding her heart. He slowly vanished away then reality kicked in so she ran to the bathroom to take a bath before her mom could get home. When she took off her underwear she noticed that she was bleeding a little, so she changed them but put back on the same clothes to avoid interrogation from her mother.

Three days had gone by, and Cmo was still on cloud 9 thinking about Eugene. She could still taste his lips, and if she reminisced long enough, she could feel his hands gliding up and down her body. She was in such a blissful fantasy that she didn't see Augustine standing in front of her with her hands behind her back. In a calm, but stern, voice, Augustine asked...

AUGUSTINE: "Are you having sex?"

Cmo looked startled, *why did she ask me that, how does she know* she thought. Cmo knew that she was going to get in trouble either way, so she lied and said

CMO: "No ma'am…"

AUGUSTINE: "You're a lie!"

CMO: "No ma'am… I'm not lying."

Then Augustine pulled the underwear out from behind her back and said…

AUGUSTINE: "Well what the hell this? I know you're not on your period!"

Augustine found Cmo's underwear with some blood and residue on them. Cmo's mother figured out that she had sex. She looked into her daughters scared eyes and something clicked inside of Augustine and she lost it. She began to beat Cmo worse than ever. She beat, whooped, beat and whooped over and over again. Cmo was beaten so badly that she couldn't go anywhere; she could barely move. Cmo's sisters were begging there mom to stop; but she wouldn't. Then once she was done with Cmo, Augustine called Eugene said to him…

AUGUSTINE: "If I even hear of you and my daughter being together like that again I will kill her and have you put in jail for it. I don't want you around her ever again."

Cmo didn't know of the conversation that Augustine had with Eugene, but she never saw or heard from Eugene again. Cmo became confused because she thought she had done something wrong to make Eugene not call her. Cmo was so hurt, Eugene lied to her all he wanted from her was sex! Eugene took her most valued treasure and left her. Those thoughts engulfed Cmo's mind, and now she hated the only person who ever really loved her. In her heart she knew he should have been her husband, the man that she would spend the rest of her life with. That sweet young man was forced out of Cmo life and she lost him forever. To make matters worse, Augustine would call her a whore and say…

AUGUSTINE: "No one would ever want someone who has been used. The person you gave it to don't even want you anymore. That's why he left your stupid ass."

Eugene and Cmo's relationship was sabotaged by her own mother and this was where Cmo's life truly fell apart.

Chapter 6

Cmo Meets William

Despite her pain of having lost her first love, Cmo started dating a slightly older man named William. She saw William as someone who could take her away from her horrific reality. She wasn't being cautious about whom she was with and she didn't care, she just needed a way out. After the loss of Eugene, life just didn't really matter anymore. William would listen to her and comfort her whenever she felt sad. He overwhelmed her with praises, complimenting her beauty, telling her that she smelt good, and showering her with gifts. He would often talk about how her life would be better if she would move in with him. Cmo was in a very vulnerable stage, and William knew it.

She began to have unprotected sex with him and eventually became pregnant. She knew that if her mother found out then [this time] she would kill her. Well, her mother did find out and she was outraged. Augustine told Cmo that she had disgraced the family by getting pregnant, and she put her out. Cmo was afraid on the streets with no place to go, so she called William to come pick her up, and he did.

Being with William seemed to be a good thing for Cmo, she was happy. She felt like she finally got the nerve to do something right in her life. A chance at being happy once again and this time she would marry this man so that he couldn't leave her. She carried this thought because she felt like she wanted to show her parent that love and unity went hand and hand.

Cmo felt her father should have left her mother and taken her with him, but he never did. Douglas stayed no matter what Augustine would say or do. To no avail, Cmo [quickly] found out that being married to William lessened her chances at happiness and peace of mind. Cmo found herself enduring a different level of abuse. She seemed to be the poster child for abuse; like her shadow, it followed her everywhere.

Chapter 7

William's Abuse

Cmo was 19 and William was 23, standing at 6'2" with black 'California curly perm' hair, pearly white teeth, freshly starched clothes, and an amazing smell. She didn't allow herself the chance to get to know William a little better. Eight months into their relationship, and a month after she moved in with him, Cmo and William got married. The wedding was a small ceremony held in his mother's back yard. Only a few people were there, and they were all his family.

Cmo communicated well with William's mother, and his mother loved her, and she showed it. They had a great relationship, something she never had with her own mother. Cmo thought it was very strange that William's mom would ask her if he'd ever gotten angry with her. But Cmo never questioned her on it, and she never questioned him either. On the day of her wedding, Cmo called a co-worker to see if she still wanted to come for the special occasion. Cmo thought it would be fine to invite one of her friends since William did not want her family to come because of their abusive history.

Cmo and William were in their room getting ready when William overheard her talking, he waited until she hung up the phone then he asked...

WILLIAM: "Who were you speaking with on the phone?"

Cmo, busy putting on her shoes, looked up from what she was doing and said...

CMO: "A co-worker."

WILLIAM: "Did you invite her?"

William inquisitively asked while on the opposite end tying his tie. Frustrated with her shoe strap, Cmo looked up once again and said...

CMO: "Yes baby, I knew you didn't want my mom and family here so I asked her to come for me?"

William turned around, this time facing Cmo and asked...

WILLIAM: "Why do you need somebody to come for you?"

By now Cmo had gotten her shoes strapped and was ready to start applying makeup. She went towards the dresser and began assembling her make up while saying…

CMO: "I just wanted a friend here with me…"

WILLIAM: "For what? Are you lonely are something? Do you miss your mom?"

CMO: "No I just wanted a friend to be here with me…Well… yes in away..."

The look on William's face sent chills throughout Cmo's body, his character changed and so did his posture. He began walking towards Cmo in slow motion, like a snake haunting its prey, his eyes turned dark and it was like looking into an evil den of destruction.

CMO: What's wrong baby?

Cmo asked, she stopped what she was doing and turned to face him.

WILLIAM: "I see I need to show you how this works."

CMO: "Huh"

Cmo was confused; had she done something wrong? Now standing over her, William said…

WILLIAM: "I told you not to be talking to people on your job…"

CMO: "What do you mean? She's just my friend…"

WILLIAM: "What do you talk to her about?"

William impatiently asked, by this time his whole body was hot with anger.

CMO: "Why?"

Cmo asked in a small voice, but that was the last comment William could take, then he exploded.

WILLIAM: "WHY!! What that fuck you mean why…Why? Because I will kill your dumb ass, that's why!"

He grabbed Cmo by her shoulders, shook her and threw her to the floor. Cmo screamed but no one came to help her. She couldn't believe that William was doing this on the day of their wedding.

WILLIAM: "Call the bitch right now and tell her not to come!"

William shouted so loudly that she felt the room move, she was so scared.

CMO: "K"

Cmo said as she got up shaking and crying, she called but there was no answer, softly she said…

CMO: "William… she not answering the phone."

WILLIAM: "Keep calling hell!"

Cmo goes to the bathroom to clean her face and apply another layer of makeup. William came in standing at 6'2" with black 'California curly perm' hair, pearly white teeth, freshly starched clothes, and smelling amazing, he looked at her through the mirror, as she looked at him through tear stained eyes, and said…

WILLIAM: "You better pray she don't come."

After those words he just walked away, and Cmo is left there starring at herself in the mirror. She, frantically, walked into the room, picked up the phone and called her friend again but still was no answer.

The wedding began and Cmo's friend has not arrived, this made Cmo happy because she didn't know what William would do if she showed up. But as her luck would have it, right before Cmo walked down the aisle, her friend showed up with guests. Cmo walked out and saw her friend and smiled towards her to show appreciation. William's posture changed once again, but with the crowd he did nothing but blow evil breaths of fire. Throughout the ceremony he held her hand, and squeezed as hard as he could. After the ceremony they began to cut the cake and serve the refreshments, Cmo was smiling gleefully, but inside she was a nervous wreck.

William began thanking the initial guest and extendedthanks in a personal way to Cmo's friend and her guests by saying…

WILLIAM: "I would like to thank allof my family and friends for coming and I want to give notice to Cmo's co-worker and her guests, we appreciate you being here."

With that, he offered them a smile and held his glass in the air; everyone cheered. Cmo was relieved, she felt as if William was sincere with his heartfelt speech.

After the ceremony, a tired Cmo and William left to go on their honeymoon. They were all smiles the entire way there, occasionally joking about the majority of their wedding guests' and their intoxicated dances. They drove for eight hours, and by the time they arrived, they were both tired and sluggish. Nevertheless, they were eager to commence their marriage, so they checked into their honeymoon suite and Cmo was the first to place her things down and she began undressing.

CMO: "I'm going to go take a shower."

WILLIAM: "Why?"

CMO: "So I can freshen up for you, baby"

Cmo said with a wink as she gave him a sexy look. William rolled his eyes and said with a grunt…

WILLIAM: "You sure?"

By this time Cmo was confused by his actions and she asked him what was wrong, but he didn't give her a straight forward answer. Cmo could see that something was bothering William so she walked over to him and placed her hands on his shoulders and said

CMO: "What baby…what's wrong?"

WILLIAM: "I mean your friend brought guests of her own. Who were those guys?"

CMO: They were just co-workers baby

Cmo said, as she began rubbing her hand across his shoulders…

WILLIAM: "WHAT"

William screamed as he jerked away from her, he grabbed her by her shoulders and pushed her across the room, and Cmo slammed; face first, into the wall.

Like before, he began walking towards her in slow motion, like a snake haunting its prey. Cmo scrambled to her feet, and pressed her body as flat as she could against the blood stained wall. He reached for her neck but she pulled away from him and ran to the other side of the wall, and that pissed him off.

WILLIAM: "Bitch, I told you NOT to do something and you did... Either you do what I ask or I'll beat your ass!"

Cmo was so confused, how had this happened? What did she do to make him mad? One minute they were laughing and joking, and the next minute her nose was bleeding and he is wailing insults at her.

CMO: "William, please tell me what is wrong? Why are you doing this to me?"

By now Cmo's eyes were red from crying, and her nose was swollen. She caught her reflection in the mirror and what she saw bought back painful memories of her abusive upbringing.

WILLIAM: "You want to know why..."

He said as he pushed her on the bed. He began to pull down her panties, spreading her legs with his face, and smelling her pussy like a dog looking for food.

WILLIAM: "...cause this pussy is mine and ain't nobody else gone have it. If it ever smells different I will fuck you up!"

He began pushing her legs apart more, spreading her open so that her legs were parallel to one another. Pain increased throughout her body, and he began to do something that he had never done before, he started licking the lips of her pussy.

CMO: "Baby I want to take a bath"

Cmo said as she tried to break free of his grip.

WILLIAM: "NO... this is my shit... if I want it dirty... so what... that's my shit!!! And this is the scent I like, so shut the fuck up and lay back"

Cmo laid back and closed her eyes, she wanted to escape, she tried to ignore the pain and then she began to feel his hands rubbing all over her body.

WILLIAM: "Don't move"

William said as he stopped to get something from out of his bag. Cmo laid there looking up at the ceiling, too scared to move in fear of what he may do to her if she did. William walked back over to the bed and in his hand ne held a long object.

WILLIAM: "You're too tight this will help loosen you up a bit."

He turned her over and began caressing her between her legs, then all of a sudden....

Cmo let out an agonizing scream as the object was shoved into her ass. William told her to shut up and hold on to the corners of the bed but she was in so much pain that she couldn't get a grip. William saw that she wasn't listening so he began to shove the object in harder and harder. Cmo started bleeding, now blood gushing from her nose and her ass, and that's when he stopped. He turned Cmo over and kissed her, apologizing for being too rough with her, and telling her that he loved her. Then he laid on top of her slid his dick into her pussy, and started moving in and out, nice and slow. Cmo, still in pain, tried to enjoy the gentleness he was displaying, which didn't last for long because he began to get excited and it got rough. By now Cmo is crying and screaming but no one could hear because William put a pillow over her face. So, Not only was she crying from pain, but now she was gasping for air. Finally, he stopped, turned over, and fell asleep; while Cmo tried to gather enough strength to breathe.

Cmo was lying next to William bleeding from both ends. She was in so much pain, but she tried to get up, if she reached the bathroom then she could soak away her pain. She managed to lean forward, but when she moved William pulled her back and said…

WILLIAM: "Suck my dick baby",

He turned her way and his dick was as hard as a rock, but she was in so much pain.

CMO: "Can I bathe first"

Anger crept back into William's eyes and he said…

WILLIAM: "What you don't want me on you, you trying to wipe my scent off you? I'll show you."

William began playing with himself, and he made Cmo watch, then he ejaculated all over Cmo and made her rub it into her skin-like lotion.

WILLIAM: "This is my scent on you bitch. Now, I said suck my mother-fucking-dick."

He slapped Cmo, and when she opened her mouth to cry out he placed his dick inside and began shoving it deep into her throat. He was getting more and more excited, so he started going faster, but she couldn't handle his excitement and she began throwing up. William, mad at her actions, began beating her, pulling on her breast, and sinking his teeth onto her flesh, giving her bite marks all over her body. The next morning he apologized and assured that it would not happen again. Everything was good for two months then life began to change.

***

William and Cmo were like two teenagers having fun. Two months into their marriage, Cmo found William's habits and behavior changing, but she didn't care because she was so happy to be away from home. William was a great provider, but she thought that the change was due to him stressing over bills because he made her quit her job. She wanted to find a way to help relieve some of the financial burden that was on his shoulders. One day she decided to ask William if she could get a job, and to her surprise, he said YES.

Cmo began working and developing new friendships with her co-workers. A month into her job, William began getting jealous and asking questions whenever Cmo would come home from work.

WILLIAM: "Where you been"

William asked one day after she came home a little late from work.

CMO: "Working baby."

Cmo said, as she put her things down and rushed over to give him a kiss.

WILLIAM: "What took you so long to get home?"

CMO: "I came home right after work."

WILLIAM: "You got here 10 minutes later than you did yesterday"

CMO: "It was more traffic today than yesterday."

WILLIAM: "Just seems a little strange."

Another month passed, and Cmo was getting off work and as she walked to her car she saw William parked in the distance. He looked at her and she smiled but he drove off, acting as though he didn't see her. When she got home he was there so she went into the house and she asked…

CMO: "Baby was that you I saw at work today parked in the parking lot?"

WILLIAM: "No, why would I be in the parking lot at your job?"

CMO: "Oh love, I just thought I saw the car, I'm sorry I guess it was just a car that looked like yours."

WILLIAM: "Why were you looking for me in your parking lot do you have something to hide."

CMO: "Oh lord, no baby I just made a mistake."

WILLIAM: "Maybe I need to come and see what man you are talking to or who is walking you to your car."

CMO: "No man walks me to my car when you're not there."

She kissed him and walked into the kitchen and began cooking dinner. Trying to move off the subject, Cmo asked…

CMO: "How was your day baby?"

WILLIAM: "I lost my damn job."

CMO: "Oh no; what happened?"

WILLIAM: "I don't want to talk about it."

CMO: "You lost your job and you don't want to talk about it?"

WILLIAM: "Yeah and!"

By now, William was screaming so Cmo just turned around and went back to peeling potatoes. They ate in silence, but the whole time Cmo was going over in her mind how she would bring up the situation without being yelled at again. After they're done eating they washed up and got ready for bed but before William came to bed he turned on the radio and cranked the music up loudly. He got into bed and began making love to Cmo. He was being a little rough, and it started hurting, so she tried slowing him down but it became more and more intense. The more she would push him away the more intense it would get. He raised her legs and spread them apart like she was doing a split, she was in excruciating pain.

Only minutes had gone by but it felt like hours to Cmo. She was drenched in sweat, but not her own. William was sweating and breathing hard like he had just ran 10 miles without stopping. By this time Cmo was screaming and crying, but no one could hear her because the music was drowning out her cries for help. The pain was so unbearable that, a pregnant Cmo, passed out while William was finishing his torture. She was awakened by the sound of the alarm clock going off the next morning. William had made her breakfast in bed scramble eggs, bacon, hash browns, pancakes with maple syrup, and orange juice. She sat up in bed and he placed the tray in front of her.

WILLIAM: "Baby I am sorry about last night, please forgive me; that will never happen again"

CMO: Yes I forgive you.

Deep in her heart, she knew that, this too, was a meaningless apology.

Cmo never knew that a man could and would abuse a woman, especially not her husband, that's why she was happy to leave home, to get away from abuse. She had never experienced abuse by the hands of a man before, nor had she ever seen it.

Cmo, after finishing what she could eat of her breakfast, went into the bathroom to take a shower and found bruises on her thighs, ankles, arms and waist where he was holding her down with so much pressure. She began to worry about the baby but all seemed to be ok. To make up for the abuse, he took her out like he had when they first moved in together. They had a great weekend, they had dinner and they watched a movie, this was something she missed for such a long time, and she loved to see him smile. Their weekend of bliss ended, and she was singing the Monday blues as she went back to work.

For lunch, William showed up at her job to take her out. She was very surprised, but it was a pleasant surprise. She had been thinking about their weekend all morning, it was nice of him to want to spend more time with her. They were eating burgers and having a great conversation when her co-workers, Steve and Anne, stopped by to say Hi. They just so happened to be eating at the same place for lunch. Cmo introduced them to her husband William and they had a few greeting words and moved on. Suddenly, the room felt cold, emotionless, unfriendly, and unkind. All laughter between the two ceased. He took her back to work and she leaned over to kiss him and he turned his head. Saying nothing, she got out of the car and he drove away without saying a word.

She went back to work, but she couldn't focus. She was in deep thought wondering what she may have done to cause him to shut down and become angry. She had introduced him to her co-workers and that was all she could think of. Nothing was said when she got home either so she cooked dinner, watched television, showered and went to bed. This silent treatment went on for the rest of the week, him only speaking when spoken too. But Friday when she got home, he was waiting for her in the bedroom with only his shorts on. When Cmo walked through the door, he said to her

WILLIAM: "Why have you been holding back on me this week?"

CMO: "We haven't had a conversation all week I thought you were upset about something."

He got up and grabbed her and threw her on the bed, he pulled down her pants and then her panties and put his face between her legs. He got back up, smelled her panties, and then put his nose back down in-between her legs again like on the night of their wedding. Then he shoved his fingers into her, tasting her natural juices to see if she tasted the same and making sure no one else came inside of her. He turned her over and looked at her ass, examining it carefully, to ensure it hadn't been touched by any other man. Cmo was terribly afraid of her husband. He became demanding, requiring a lot of time, attention, and energy from Cmo. Cmo had to endure it all because she had nowhere else to go. He knew she couldn't go home to her mother because he knew all about her family's history of abuse.

This was the crutch he would lean on whenever she would threaten to leave he'll say WILLIAM: "Your own mother hates you, seems like you would be used to the beatings, you grew up with a crazy momma, nobody else will love you like I do."

Cmo knew she'd made a mistake marrying him, if only she wasn't so heartbroken, then this would have never happened. She allowed herself to run right into the arms of an abusive man. But she didn't know about his abusive ways. While she was seeing him and living at home with her mother he was a loving man. Even though she would be abused by William, she thought she had to stay with him because she didn't have a family to go home to. She hadn't called or spoken to any of her family members for months.

She felt that her family didn't love her anyway. He started to beat her at least twice a week. She had blackened eyes from time to time, bruises on her skin, and sprained fingers, which prevented her from working. Her arm was [also] broken and she began to call into work because of her scars; inside and out. Cmo lost her job because of her lack of attendance and she was unable to focus because William had her so terrified. With her job gone, now no one was working and William was furious. He began to look for work and she asked again if she may look for work but this time he told her NO. She was, now, back into the position that she was in before; whatever is done in the household, William would have the final say and her thoughts no longer mattered.

Chapter 8

William's Son

William found somewhere to work and he was on his job for a little over a week, when he came in from work one day with a little boy. The little boy was a sweet child. He said to Cmo that since she wasn't working she could help the mother of this child out by keeping him while she worked. Cmo thought that maybe she would be a babysitter for the child's mother while getting paid for the work. Cmo, now six months pregnant, had been keeping this child for two weeks when she finally asked.

CMO: "How much will the lady be paying me to watch her child and when".

William backed her up into a corner, starring her down and screaming

WILLIAM: "How you gone ask the mother of my child to pay you for keeping my son"

This was the first time William ever told her he had a son. Cmo was a stepmother and she didn't even know it. This was also, the first time Cmo found out that her husband was married before her. His son was in the room when he yelled at Cmo and the boy [Domino] began to cry.

WILLIAM: "Shut the hell up boy, I'll whoop your ass"

William yelled at his son, who was only six, but he quickly hushed. William never wanted Cmo to meet his ex-wife but one day she came to pick Domino up. William worked late that evening so Domino's mother informed Cmo in a conversation, that if she [Cmo] wasn't apart of William's life, then he [Domino] would probably never see his father. She told Cmo that because he was so abusive towards her, she didn't trust him and his temper around her son.

When they were married William beat her while she was pregnant and she almost lost Domino. Cmo and the William's ex-wife shared so much, but after their conversation, Cmo became even more afraid for her life and the life of her baby. Domino's mother didn't bring him around anymore because of all the bruises she saw on Cmo and also because her son began to flinch whenever she would scold him. But of course, William blamed Cmo because it was the day that she picked the child up, and he wasn't there to see her so she never came back.

Chapter 9

Birth of the First Child

Cmo now seven months pregnant, alone, and afraid with no one to talk to [also] her 20th birthday was coming up. She had been isolated from everyone she knew. So she prayed to God, for William to allow her to go to church, so she could see her old classmates and church friends. Her birthday would be on the Wednesday coming up and that Saturday, the week before, Cmo cooked a very good meal thinking if she made sure that he remained happy maybe he would let her do something nice for her birthday.

Sunday was a great day and she felt even more comfortable. Monday when Williams came home, to her surprise, William asked her what she would like to do for her birthday. Beaming with happiness because her prayers had been answered, she nervously said…CMO: "I would like to go to church."

William looked at her inquisitively and said…

WILLIAM: "Church?"

Cmo knew that her next sentence would have to be said carefully because she didn't want to stir his temper so she said…

CMO: "Yes, we haven't been in a while. I just want to go to church for my birthday."

WILLIAM: "Ok baby",

William said as he walked over to her gently putting his arms around her

WILLIAM: "I love you and if that is what you want then that's what we'll do."

CMO: "Oh, thank you so much I love you too"

***

Wednesday morning Cmo awakened with a smile on her face, she prayed that nothing would go wrong today, she wanted it all to be perfect. But William, who has more mood swings then a teenager going through puberty, was subjected to coming home pissed off at the world for no reason. Cmo cooked a wonderful dinner, his favorite meal, and when William came home, unexpectedly, he was in a very good mood. Cmo was standing in the kitchen with a spoon in her hand when he came in with a big smile on his face and said…

WILLIAM: "Hey baby"

CMO: "Hello love, how was your day"

Cmo said as she hugged him and mumbled a *thank you Jesus* under her breath.

WILLIAM: "It was a great day, How about you? What have you been doing birthday girl?"

CMO: "I've been preparing dinner for you baby, and getting things ready for tonight."

WILLIAM: "You got kitty ready for me I want desert before dinner tonight and again later on."

With a smirk, he kneels slightly and began to put his hand between her legs and kissed her lips then moving down to her breast. Rubbing on her body gently and saying softly…

WILLIAM: "I love you and I want to give you a good birthday gift".

Cmo was thinking *well there goes church*, as she's puts the spoon down and under her breath asks God "Why". Of course she was going to have sex with him, because if not, he would get so mad that he would beat her.

CMO: "I love you too and I will give you what you want baby"

Cmo said this,but secretly hoping this would go quickly so that they will still have time for church. She tried to separate because his grip was really tight but, he pulled her back gently and brought her down to his level and slowly leaned her back to the floor and whispered in her ear…

WILLIAM: "I want desert that means right here, on the kitchen floor." Smirking again, he began going down on her and when he finished he asked…

WILLIAM: "What's for dinner"?

William left to wash his face and hands and he came back to the dinner table that had been set with a beautiful table cloth, special place settings, and some flowers.

WILLIAM: "This looks great babe"

William said as he sat down, eagerly awaiting his second portion.

CMO: "I just wanted it special for us baby"

WILLIAM: "Yeah, baby you have been through so much I want your birthday to be very special for you"

William said as he playfully pulled her down onto his lap.

"Yeah, you have already made that possible."

William stopped for a second and looked at her and asked…

WILLIAM: "What do you mean?"

CMO: "I mean all that loving you just gave me baby"

Cmo said in a loving tone, trying not to upset him.

WILLIAM: "Oh, it was good to you huh."

CMO: "Mmmhhmmm".

He got quiet and they finished up dinner, afterwards, he wanted to take a shower together. By now, it was seven o'clock church will began at seven thirty. *Great* she thought but before she left the kitchen she asked...

CMO: "Do you want me to do the dishes before we shower or after?"

WILLIAM: "No more cleaning for you on your birthday. I will get those when we get back from church."

Wow! Cmo thought...*This is great, the change on his part, was it really happening?* Cmo was so elated, that she gleamed with joy. As they showered, he kissed her with so much passion and this was the first time [in a long time] she felt any kind of sexual emotion for him. Cmo thought that he was going to want to have more sex and delay church even further, but it didn't happen. They got out of the shower and he rubbed her stomach for the first time and the baby kicked, hard.

WILLIAM: "What the hell."

CMO: "He's just full from dinner and may have fallen asleep and the shower woke him up."

WILLIAM: "He's a strong little man huh"

CMO: "Just like his daddy."

***

They arrived to church an hour late but it didn't matter because Cmo was just so excited to be there that she didn't care if they arrived two hours late, just as long as she was able to go. William allowed Cmo to pick the section where she wanted to sit, so she chose the middle aisle.

Cmo thought this would be a central location to ensure that she wasn't sitting next to anyone she knew, so that William wouldn't get angry with her. William seemed to be having a great time. He stood when they sang and even said Amen to some of the things the minister said. It was time for the offering and Cmo reached into her purse to get the only ten dollars that she had. She saved this ten dollar bill over a period of two months because William would monitor the money she spent or any change she would get after a purchase. But most of the ten came from when he would go to work and leave her 50cents for a soda. William never said a word, they walked around the table and different ones were speaking and waving because they hadn't seen them in about four or five months.

They were all so happy to see them, and so was Cmo. After church was over, one of Cmo's friends called her over and began talking with her, William just stood there looking. Cmo was so excited to be around friends, that she began holding long conversations and laughing. They were surprised to see that she was pregnant and some of them rubbed her belly and she laughed. Each time one of the ladies would touch her belly, the baby would kick and they would laugh. She looked at William and he gestured for her to come to him. Nodding in agreement, she began walking towards him, and then someone else stepped into her path so she began walking and talking at the same time until she reached William.

WILLIAM: "Let's GO!"

CMO: "OK baby."

Cmo said with a smile, but she knew something was wrong. So many people were trying to talk to her, but they were rushing out of the door, until one of the deacons walked up to William and said...

DEACON: "How you doing Brother William?"

WILLIAM: "Fine Deacon"

William said, trying to walk around him, but there were people blocking the narrow aisle, so he had no choice but to stay.

DEACON: "We miss you Brother, when are you coming back?"

WILLIAM: "We are back. This is our new beginning."

Cmo stood next to him smiling, happy to hear those words come out of William's mouth. In the meantime, William, holding her hand, sees her smiling and looked at her and said...

WILLIAM: "Bitch what you smiling at."

He began squeezing her hand tighter until it was difficult for her to continue holding his hand. So, she pretended someone was calling and she turned quickly to separate herself from him; but she never moved from his presence. William and Deacon were still conversing and Cmo could tell he wanted to end the conversation so William kindly said...

WILLIAM: "Deacon I must get my wife home she's tired and I will be talking with you on Sunday, Lords will and say the same."

DEACON: "All right my brother until then."

The conversation with the Deacon was different from the actions she was receiving from her husband and the words that were coming out of his mouth. William opened the car door for Cmo she got in he walked around to the opposite side, he got in, and they drove off. Cmo watched as the church disappeared from the rearview mirror. Driving for about three minutes in silence, all of a sudden, "BAM" Cmo was slapped across her face with as much strength as William could muster. Cmo's head hit the passenger side window and cracked it. Cmo didn't see a light; she only saw Hell's doors open up with unnerving, terrifying fear.

WILLIAM: "That was for giving my ten dollars to another man."

SLAP!

WILLIAM: "That's for waving at those men when we went around that DAMN offering table."

He reached back over and punched her on the arm, POP!

WILLIAM: "That's for walking away from me."

Now she was balled up in a fetal position, screaming and crying...

CMO: "I'm sorry, I'm sorry."

WILLIAM: "Bitch shut the FUCK up! I'll kill your stupid ass!"

CMO: "Why, Why please stop." Cmo screamed

WILLIAM: "Why you let those Bitches touch my baby! And you were smiling the whole time. Bitch you crazy if you think that's ok."

Cmo started throwing up in the car and that just pissed him off even more. He stopped the car and got out and crossed over to the passenger's side and pulled Cmo out of the car. He pushed her to her knees and pressed her face into the mud. He said

WILLIAM: "Eat dirt Bitch this is for throwing up in my damn car. You're gonna clean that shit up. Get back in the damn car Bitch."

She struggled to get up, but he was impatient and he yanked her arm. Hearing her bones break, he didn't care he continued to pull on it, throwing her into the back seat of the car. He drove off like a bat out of Hell and before they made it home, she passed out. Cmo faintly heard his voice as she regained consciousness. She tried to stand but he got tired of waiting and again pulled her out of the car, into the house, and up onto the couch, by her broken arm. All the while, she was screaming from the pain, William said…

WILLIAM: "Shut the fuck up Bitch! Shut up!"

Cmo tried focusing, but she couldn't see anything so he slapped her in her mouth and some of her teeth flew across the room. She tried to look at him but her eyes and mouth were swollen and bloody. She could hardly part her eyes but tears of blood continued streaming down her face. She was barely able to sit up, but William didn't care so he told her

WILLIAM: "Stand up get in front of me... Come on shit, I don't have all night... I work in the morning."

Cmo was trying very hard to remember what she had done to make him so mad; standing in front of him she asked

CMO: "What did I do?"

Her mouth was so swollen that she couldn't even make out her own words.

POW! He slapped her again...

WILLIAM: "Bitch you know what the hell you did? Don't act so damn dumb with your stupid ass!"

CMO: "What"

WILLIAM: "Why were you letting all those men hug you and the Deacon when we left!?

CMO: "It didn't mean anything, I was just being friendly."

WILLIAM: "I will kill you! I don't want anybody touching you. You hear me?"

He pushed her up and she hit the wall, back first, and when she leaned forward he picked her up and body slammed her down to the floor like a wrestler. On the floor, he pulled her dress up, ripped her panties off, rolled her over, and began to rape her. She was screaming for God or anyone to help her, but he kept going and going; grunting like a gorilla. A broken arm, broken jaw, swollen mouth, and being brutally raped, caused enough pain for one night, she surrendered to her injuries and passed out.

WILLIAM: "Get your ass up and take a shower!"

She opened her eyes just enough to see William kicking her, but she was in so much pain that she couldn't feel it because her whole body was aching. The house was eerily dark and she could hardly see with both eyes swollen, not able to get up, she crawled to the bathroom.

WILLIAM: "Crawl Bitch crawl. You're crawling like a damn dog. Your mom said you were a dog. I see it's true."

William said while he laughed evilly. Cmo got into the shower holding and leaning on to the wall for support. She saw blood when she wiped her vagina and when she wiped her butt. She was thinking that the blood she saw was only there because he raped her. He had always been rough with her and whenever that occurred, as often as it did, she would pass out.

This became a routine in their sex life; she felt that William liked it when she passed out because she would be sore all over when she regained consciousness. William took advantage of her while she was passed out. She snapped back to reality after feeling the cold water on her bare skin. She climbed out of the shower and went into the living room; he came in and sweetly said…

WILLIAM: "Come to bed baby."

She walked slowly to the bedroom, and he helped her into bed and said…

WILLIAM: "I don't know why you do the things you do to make me crazy. Girl I love you and I don't want to hurt you but you just piss me off sometimes. I am so sorry this will never happen again."

She laid down thinking...*What should I do? If I don't leave then this man will kill me and my baby.* As he lay next to her, he began to cuddle her like a baby in his arms. Meanwhile, her arm was broken, eyes bloodshot and swollen shut, and she was bleeding from her vagina and her anus. Before she drifted off to sleep, she prayed to God asking him for a way out of this [horrific] situation.

The next morning William got up to go to work, as Cmo rolled over she noticed him coming out of the bathroom dressed and ready to go.

WILLIAM: "I put you some food on the dresser don't come out of this room, don't try to call nobody, don't go outside and don't try to leave; I will find you and kill you and the baby."

CMO: "OK"

Cmo said as tears flow down her face. She thought back to when they first moved in, she could remember him putting a dead bolt lock on the bedroom door, but he'd never used it. Today he locked her in with that same deadbolt lock, so she couldn't escape. They lived on the second floor and there wasn't another way out. She was sitting up on the bed, though it was hard to move, she got up and opened the window because it was very hot in the room. She leaned out to get some fresh air and she began to think *I can get out through the window.*

As quickly as her tattered body could move, she gathered some sheets and curtains and tied them together the best that she could with a freshly broken arm. She opened the closet door and began to throw all the clothes out of the window as if to build a tower so that her fall would be cushioned. She tied one end of the sheet in a huge knot and placed it in the closet and closed the door leaving the knot behind the door, she was determined to leave. She wrapped part of the sheet around the leg of the bed and threw the other end of the window. Then in excruciating pain, with one hand, she lowered herself as far as she could to the ground and fell to safety.

She began walking, not knowing where to go, she was deliriously walking. Nearly getting hit by cars; she was determined to find help. She found herself on a familiar street after walking for about three hours, but still in and out of deliria. Her father drove by and glanced at his rearview mirror.

Is that my baby? He thought to himself, and then he looked harder and recognized that it was Cmo.

DOUGLAS: "OH SHIT!"

He came to a screeching halt. He backed up and got out of his car and looked at his baby and began to cry, he put her into the car and took her home. Douglas was trying to get her to talk but she was non-responsive, like she was in complete and utter shock.

DOUGLAS: "Baby talk to me... Who did this...? Were you raped...? Where's William, does he know? How long you been walking? Oh, my God... Please help us... I'll get you home baby... just hold on."

Douglas drove up the driveway blowing his horn profusely, as he opened the garage door, Augustine, franticly, ran out to the car to see what was wrong.

AUGUSTINE: "What's wrong baby?"

DOUGLAS: "It's Cmo!"

AUGUSTINE: "Cmo?! What happened baby?"

Douglas ran to the opposite side of the car and opened the front passenger door, reached in, and picked up Cmo's limped body.

AUGUSTINE: "Oh my God my baby! Douglas what happened?"

DOUGLAS: "I don't know I found her like this."

AUGUSTINE: "What! Found her?!"

DOUGLAS: "Yes baby, she was walking about five miles down the street."

AUGUSTINE: "Baby what happen to you?"

Tears began rolling down Augustine's face as she looked at Cmo's unresponsiveness.

Douglas carried her up the stairs to her old room, Augustine followed close behind, sobbing hysterically saying…

AUGUSTINE: "That's my baby. That boy beat her up. Jesus, she is so messed up. Please spare my child."

Cmo was confused, she couldn't remember how she got to her mama's house, but she remembered her mama saying "That's my baby." Cmo's family took care of her. Even though she was a rebellious and bad child, her mama showed her love in her time of need. She prayed for her, fed her, and bathed her. Cmo hadn't seen her parents since Augustine put her out, but Douglas never knew she was pregnant. On a Thursday night, she was in the room with her mom and her eldest sister telling them what she had been going through and what happened the night before. She started to hurt really badly so she told her sister

CMO: "Please pray for me my stomach hurts so badly. I don't want to lose my baby."

Her stomach was hurting her terribly, but she tried not to let it show, she told them that she wanted to get some rest so they left her alone. Right after the door closed, Cmo began to pray...

CMO: "Jesus, please don't let me lose my baby."

Cmo's mother came back up stairs and asked her if she needed anything and Cmo said that she may need help going to the bathroom. She leaned over because she couldn't get up on her own and her mother began to help her, while helping her daughter she saw blood all over the bed where Cmo was sitting. Her mom yelled for her father to come up stairs...

116

AUGUSTINE: "Douglas! We have to take her to the hospital!"

Her dad rushed up the stairs and immediately picked her up and carried her down stairs, put her in the car, and they drove to the hospital. Cmo had her hand between her legs pressing, and holding tightly. She didn't know that she was holding her baby boy's head. They arrived at the hospital and the nurse told her to let go of the grip she had on her unborn child; but she was afraid to let go.

CMO: "He may fall out; I got to keep him in. It's too early"

NURSE: "How far along are you?"

CMO: "Seven…Ohhhh this hurts. I am seven months. I don't want to let him go, Lord, Jesus, I don't want to let him go."

NURSE: "Ma'am you've got to move your hand"

The nurse said as she tried to see if the baby was crowning.

CMO: "I can't. He's right here. I can't let him go."

The nurse gently removed her hand, and what she saw frightened her.

NURSE: "The baby's head."

The nurse gasped, and she quickly rushed to find a doctor. As her baby entered into the world, Cmo lost consciousness. The pain from her injuries coupled with the birth of her son, was more than what Cmo's fragile body could withstand. But in the room, there wasn't any crying, any joy, and no happiness. The baby was stillborn. Entering this world on the same day as Augustine and Douglas's anniversary, Cmo's baby boy named Chris, died by the hands of his abusive father.

When Cmo regained consciousness, she sat up and started looking around the room trying to see her baby. She wanted to hold him, and kiss him, and tell him how much she loved him. But the doctor walked in empty handed, and he was saying something to her, but she wasn't listening.

CMO: "Where's my baby" she said, eagerly wanting nothing more than to stare into his beautifully perfect eyes, she imagined that he'd have eyes like hers. The doctor looked at her and with sympathy in his voice, he said…

DOCTOR: "Did you hear anything that I have explained to you? It looks like your baby was fighting in your womb because he had bruises. He must have twisted himself until the umbilical cord wrapped around his little neck. That, coupled with the domestic abuse you've endured, was what caused his death."

Death, that is the only word Cmo comprehended. Death is that dreadful word that could leave a void in the midst of eternal happiness. Her son, her baby boy, had fallen victim to Death, so what was the point of life.

She began sobbing bitterly, not only for her baby, but also for herself. How could she have endured that abuse for so long? Her baby fought for life until the end, he was a survivor, just like his mommy. Afterwards, she became very silent, never uttering a word. She didn't know of the abuse, the other wife, the child, his jealousy, or how he was in his past relationships before she married him. She just wanted out of her mother's house.

People are sometimes able to hide their abusiveness on their own or with the help of others. Had his mother spoken to her about his actions in the past, maybe Cmo would not have faced this abusive behavior from her husband. All families have history. Make sure to ask around, investigate, and listen to that still small voice within your mind; it could be a warning from God.

Cmo sat in silence and began to think... *His mother never told me that he was abusive, why didn't she warn me. I wonder if she was beaten by William's father. Was she afraid for her life? She was married when she was 20 years old, she knows how it feels to endure such pain, why keep this from me. They lied to me; NO, I was manipulated and misused. He falsified his image, forged an altered lifestyle, and tampered with my heart.* Cmo felt like she was in love but found herself in the clutches of an abuser's arms. So many thoughts began running through Cmo's head.

DOUGLAS: "Baby come home till you feel better and let us take care of you."

But Cmo said nothing.

William's abuse led to the death of their child. 'Death by father' is what they should've written on his death certificate, but they were kind enough to put 'Premature Death'. Cmo had lost her first born and had become very bitter. She missed her son; she wanted to feel him move inside of her once again. She wanted to hear his heartbeat, and feel him press up against her hand whenever she rubbed her belly. To lose a child can and will always be devastating.

No one really knew how Cmo felt, she allowed those feelings to fester inside of her, yeah she changed and she knew it. She began acting as if nothing happened or nothing was wrong. However, she loved her son very much and began plotting her revenge. She would always speak to herself, saying, *I wonder what his life would have been like. Where would he be now? Would he have gone to college? Oh God, I wonder what my baby would have become today. Chris I love and I miss you but mommy will avenge your death.*

It's so hard to lose a child, even if that child is lost in the womb. You carry that living being inside of you for, hopefully, nine months. Therefore, in reality your body becomes that child's home supplied with food and beverage, transportation, clothing, education, and development. You eat to nourish the child, you go to the doctor to ensure a healthy formation of the child, the clothing is your body to protect the child from hot, cold and insure a safe environment. To read, sing and talk with your unborn child is to broaden his or her learning abilities and the developing process is the combination of all of the above.

The umbilical cord is what connects mother to child. Even though, after birth the umbilical cord is cut. The mother and child will always be connected; for the reason "She gave life to her beloved child". So truly we are all grateful for our mothers because they endured the pain to have us and gave us life.

124

Chapter 10

Cmo Goes Back To William

William began calling Cmo and Cmo would talk to him against her parents' wishes. Cmo had a plan [this is going to sound strange] Cmo, eventually, went back to William after he brutally abused her and killed their son. However, she wasn't going back to be with him, she went back for revenge. Hatred was in her heart and it made her whole outlook on life change. They were happy [so he thought] but Cmo only went back because she was going to do something to him to make him feel the pain that she felt for the loss of her baby.

Chris was her only child, and the love of her life. While at home, Cmo had so many bad thoughts of how he treated her before and now he's just being nice, but she refused to let her guard down this time. She was ready to avenge her son's death, by any means necessary. *He really loves my cooking* Cmo thought, so she decided that she was going to make him a good meal, and then she was going to leave. She went to the store and she bought his favorite meal neck bones, sweet potatoes, spinach, and some hot water cornbread. When she got home he began to question her about where she'd been and who she saw. *Not this shit again;* Cmo thought to herself, *I just went to the damn store.* Cmo's silence began making William even angrier. So he walked over to her and grabbed hold of her arm, squeezing it tightly.

CMO: "You said you wouldn't do this anymore…"

WILLIAM: "Why did you go to the store without me?"

CMO: "You said you wouldn't do this to me anymore..."

Her voice was very calm, but the anger inside her had not subsided. William didn't know that he was dealing with an angry [distraught] woman whose manifested hatred derived from the person standing before her. But yet and still, he continued holding on to her arm, squeezing it tighter, but he noticed that she didn't flinch. *What the hell,* William thought to himself, *Oh, she want to act all big and bad, well I got something for that.* He slapped her but she just stood there, she did not fall, she stood firm. So he slapped her again, this time even harder, but her expression and demeanor was the same.

Though he slapped her with all of his power, she showed no reflection of emotion because the pain in her heart was far greater than the pain on her face. She pushed him, with every ounce of strength in her body and with every bit of anger in her heart, she pushed him. Shocked by the strength that Cmo displayed, William bounced against the wall and fell to the floor.

The room began moving in slow motion; Cmo reached behind the refrigerator and pulled out the gun she had hidden for the past six weeks she'd been there. She turned around to shoot but he grabbed her leg and she fell with the gun still in her hand, it went off, shooting her in the leg.

Though she'd just been shot, she didn't feel a thing; she pulled the trigger again and the bullet hit William in the arm. Adrenaline pumping, she began shooting, and she shot and shot until he stopped moving. After shooting him, Cmo turned around and looked at the stove; she grabbed the pot of steaming sweet potatoes and began pouring it on his face. Then she picked up the pot of boiling neck bones and dumped it all over the front of his pants. Now satisfied, Cmo said…

CMO: "Here's your dinner Bitch."

Not having a phone, she walked over to the neighbor's house and called the police to report that someone had been shot. The police were familiar with her address so they came over thinking that it was Cmo who had gotten shot, but to their surprise, it was Cmo who they had sitting in the back seat of the police car. Cmo, was elated and she said to the police…

CMO: "I whooped that ass, I'm not proud of it but I whooped his ass because I was tired of it."

She was taken to the county jail but they released her because it was self-defense. William was shot three times and had extensive burns to his face and genitals, but he survived.

The lesson here was, it's not wrong to fight, but I'm not saying it's right to stand there and take it either. Basically, I'm saying she should not have gone back. Her ties should have been cut when he murdered her child and severely beat her up. Now because of her going back and nearly killing her husband in the process; she had become a bitter person with trust and emotional issues on top of an anger problem. Revenge is not the solution, neither is it the antidote for a broken heart. If you want to begin healing you must first learn to forgive.

Cmo began the process of filing for a divorce from William and found out that she had to wait eight months before the divorce would be final. Unexpectedly, after Cmo was released from jail she became ill. Thinking that it was food poisoning; she went to the doctor and actually found out that she was four weeks pregnant. Her parents allowed her to stay with them, and that was where she stayed and had a healthy baby girl named Patience.

Cmo named her daughter Patience to remind herself of the emotional action that she should always display, so that she will never turn into Augustine. Cmo was happy, she started to get her life back together, she had a beautiful daughter who loved her dearly, and as for the icing on the cake- her divorce was final.

Cmo found a good job where she was able to buy a car and eventually move into her own apartment. She began to live again with an appreciation for life and love of her daughter. The relationship that she maintained with

Patience was very different than that of hers and her mother. Cmo swore to herself and God that she would not be bringing up her child in an abusive environment.

Patience was now different than that of hers, and her mother. Ono swore to herself and God that she would not be bringing up her child in an abusive environment.

Chapter 11

Cmo and Steve

About a year after her divorce, Cmo became interested in a young man named Steve. Steve was calm, pleasant, and romantic he was also a real gentleman towards Cmo and Patience. Steve and Augustine were acquainted; she even expressed how much she felt he was a good match for Cmo. Steve and Cmo began dating and their feelings matured for one another, they were falling in love.

After being together for nearly a year, they decided to get married. By now Patience was two and they wanted to have another baby right away so, shortly after, Cmo became pregnant. While pregnant she began to notice a difference in Steve's actions. They were not going out or conversing like they did before her pregnancy. Steve began to sleep a lot and became an annoyance. There weren't any sexual relations between the two, and Cmo thought it was because she had put on a few too many pounds while pregnant.

One day Cmo decided to ask Steve what turned him off in their relationship because it was not the same as before.

CMO: "Baby"

STEVE: "Yeah"

CMO: "What has happened with our relationship... our marriage...?"

STEVE: "Nothing baby... I've just been tired lately."

CMO: "Is that it? Your eyes have been really red are you getting enough sleep?"

STEVE: "Yes, baby... It's just... Well... I don't know how to really tell you this"

CMO: "What baby? Just tell me... Is it someone else?"

STEVE: "No, nothing like that...I don't know how you're going to take this, but…I smoke."

CMO: "Smoke? We've been together for three years... I never knew you smoked?"

STEVE: "Yes I do and I just didn't know how you would take it."

CMO: "I don't care baby as long as it is not around the children?"

STEVE: "I won't ever smoke around the kids. But I don't think you understand?"

CMO: "What?"

STEVE: "I smoke... MJ"

CMO: "WHAT!?"

Steve informed her of his addictive habit of smoking marijuana (MJ). He stated that he had been smoking MJ, subsequently, before they met and was a continuous smoker ever since. Steve had such a bad habit of smoking marijuana that he would steal to support his habit. It had gotten so bad that Cmo couldn't take it anymore; he was neglecting his responsibilities and putting his family at risk.

Even though he never laid a finger on her, he was displaying some form of abuse.

His habit worsened and he began to primo his marijuana with cocaine. Cmo began to see that this was another abusive relationship, but tried very hard to make her marriage work. After the birth of her third child Peace, Cmo sat down and had a talk with her husband where she begged him to stop for the family's sake. Steve promised her he would, however, he never stopped.

On the day of his mother's 50th birthday party, the children were at the sitter's and they were getting ready for the celebration. Cmo was very nervous about attending this party. Steve's parents and family began to dislike her because Steve seemed to lose his edge after they got married and they blamed her. Steve's family didn't know that he was using drugs.

Cmo became very upset because she was being blamed for the down fall of their family and she wasn't the one causing the problems. His addiction caused a lack in income, because he'd lost his job. Cmo became the soul bread winner for the family but she knew that she would hear negative comments coming from Steve's family with all fingers pointed towards her.

STEVE: "Let me blow some of this smoke into your face and it will calm you down."

CMO: "No way! I don't want to inhale that stuff..."

STEVE: "You won't be smoking it so it's cool…Look I'm just going to blow and you take a deep breath."

CMO: "It won't hurt me?"

STEVE: "No baby... I will never hurt you…"

CMO: "Ok"

Cmo inhaled as Steve blew, and after a while, Cmo began feeling very differently. Not understanding this feeling, she laid down to gather herself, but Steve kept blowing. The room started smelling differently and she became very horny her heart began racing and her breathing increased. Her body was becoming restless and anxious, they began to have sex. Steve had gotten her high on marijuana laced with crack cocaine. The night ended with them both smoking crack cocaine out of a pipe.

Cmo had now become addicted along with Steve and this addiction went on for almost 7 months. Peace, now nine months and Patience, Cmo's eldest daughter, was nearly four years old; this was when Cmo got the nerve to stop.

She made the decision to move into her own apartment; neither of the girls' fathers were doing anything to help out, so she didn't think she needed to stay around. She tried everything to get the dads to come see their children, but William was too stubborn and Steve was strung out on drugs.

One day Steve came over to see the children and Cmo noticed that every time he'd visit, they would have sex; she only did it because she knew that it encouraged him to return. One day Cmo awakened to find herself next to Steve and she vowed to herself that this too shall stop. This type of behavior gave her the feeling of being a prostitute for the sake of her children, even though it was with men she was previously married to (yes married to, she was doing the same with William).

Cmo wanted desperately for the fathers of her children to step up and be in their lives. Teaching them to love their fathers had nothing to do with her relationship with them. The one thing that was consistent between Cmo and her parents were the fact that they were a family, yes with an illness, but still a family no doubt.

Cmo knew the importance of family and was yet trying to instill her moral values within her children. She found herself trading sexual favors in exchange for time spent between her children and their fathers. Actually, the fathers never came unless they knew she was going to let them have sex with her. Cmo would have sex with them anyway, because she liked it, but she also thought it was her duty. But one day she had an epiphany, having sex with these men in order for her children to see them was morally wrong. This immoral act went on for a year with both fathers and it became another form of abuse in Cmo's life, self-abuse. These guys would never call to check on their children, they would only call to see if they could come and lay with her.

Cmo decided to move on with her life instead of living in a past of negative experiences. She progressed in taking on a positive role of parenting, this decision brought about a change in both fathers' lives.

Cmo hoped that one day these fathers would come through and start helping her with their children. She thought that they would become responsible parents. She longed for the day when God would put something in their hearts and minds to remind them that they [each] have a child. So she devised a plan that would, hopefully, result in the girls seeing the error of their fathers' ways. Cmo thought that if she moved away, the excuse used would be better for her children. She felt like her plan would stop the prostitution and cause the truth to be revealed. But if she moved, she knew the children would not see their fathers but it was a choice that had to be made. Still, these were a few questions Cmo was faced with:

1. Do I continue to prostitute for my children, so that they could see their fathers? Lying to the children, having them think their fathers are there for them and knowing in my heart of hearts that they just want my lips and what is between my legs (a blow job and a wet pussy)
2. Is polishing the loins of a man worth the deception of a child learning that their absentee parent doesn't want to be a part of their lives and teach them how to deal with the loss of a parent even though said parent is alive?

These two questions can result in a lifetime of pain for all involved. Cmo had taken on both fathers' responsibilities in order to give her children peace of mind. But then again, she needed a way out of this unhealthy relationship she had [unconsciously] placed herself, her ex-husbands, and her children into.

This was where her thoughts began to come into focus. She felt that if she put a little distance between them, it would be a better excuse used for the girls instead of the fathers being there and never coming to see them. So she decided to put somewhat of a cushion between them, one that would display the truth to strengthen her foundation with her children.

The foundation that she is building for the children, at this point, is of an unhealthy relationship; it is built on lies and deception. Remember her original foundation was in question because of the illness of abuse within it. Cmo is finding that abuse follows her but in different forms. She feels that she knows what is best for the establishment of her children. Understanding that she will make mistakes but not caring because of the love she feel she needs because she doesn't, exactly, know what love truly is.

She, unconsciously, began making excuses for their fathers for the first three to five years of her children's life. Then she realized that they were living in the same city, just around the corner, and still didn't come to see them nor help out. With that in mind, what would be the difference in this situation? The only difference was that she was helping them acquire excuses that were relevant.

Chapter 12

Cmo and Steve's Divorce

During the process of her divorce from Steve, Cmo received an offer to work in Chicago, Illinois. This was the reason she was struggling with her decision of whether to stay or go. But time was of the essence, and she wanted a fresh start, so she decided to accept the offer and they moved to Chicago. In her divorce decree it was stated that she would pay for the children to visit their father, and the father would pay for the children to return home. No sooner after their divorce was final, Steve remarried. One evening, after not contacting or hearing from him for months, Steve called…

STEVE: "Hello Cmo."

CMO: "Hello Steve how are you?"

STEVE: "I'm good; I'm calling to check on the children."

CMO: "Oh... well they're here and doing fine, would you like to speak with them?" (Feeling as if a change was coming, he had called her for the first time and literally asked about the children without any sexual dialect, even his tone was different).

STEVE: "Yes I would like to speak with them, but I must let you know that I am married now and I want to start spending more time with them. My wife has children and I want them to know each other."

CMO: "Wow, Steve that is great. Ok, hold on let me go get them for you."

Thanking God within her heart, because she felt that her children were going to begin a healthy relationship with their father without her having to compromise her position. It had finally happened; the children were going to feel the effects of a healthy family relationship. The children haven't seen either of their fathers in two years. Cmo called each of them to the phone to inform them of who was on the phone. Of course they were ecstatic because of the healthy thoughts Cmo kept in their heads, "Your daddies love you, give them time they will call; they are very busy etc..."Steve made BIG promises to the girls and they planned their trip to their father's house.

That summer, Cmo drove her children down to Cameron, Pennsylvania to see Steve. When Cmo arrived, she was surprised to see that Steve's wife and step-children were not home. That was a part of the plan, Cmo was supposed to meet the woman who would have her babies for three weeks. Cmo looked past the issue because she thought that she would meet them before she left.

The children were so excited and Cmo was thrilled that the reunion was going well between them. She had so much on her mind, both good and bad, then Steve's wife arrived, but there weren't any children with her. Steve introduced the two, and Cmo shrugged off the suspicious feeling. She was ready to let her babies have their time with their daddy, so she provided instructions on the medications and other issues that may arise, then she gave them each a hug and kiss good-bye. As Cmo walked out of the house she heard Steve make a statement to his wife...

STEVE: "Stay with the kids I want to talk with Cmo and make sure I have all the information needed."

HIS WIFE: "Ok, no problem."

STEVE: "Ok baby, I will be right back."

CMO: "Ok y'all mamma will see y'all in three weeks. Oh yeah... Steve have you decided if they are flying, or will you, the wife and children be bringing them back?"

STEVE: "We're going to bring them back, just the wife and me; we should be there by that Friday."

CMO: "Great, Ok girls y'all hear that, you have three weeks with daddy, enjoy!"

Steve and Cmo stood outside the house and the children stayed in the house with Steve's wife. Cmo was giving Steve her work number when Steve asked...

STEVE: "When are you going back home from this trip?"

CMO: "Oh, I am leaving now I just came to bring them to you."

STEVE: "What about us?"

CMO: "Us?"

STEVE: "Yeah... us. What have we always done? I miss that."

CMO: "Damn... are you serious?"

STEVE: "Yeah baby, I miss you this is why I wanted you to come you know that."

CMO: "No I didn't know that, but know this, that is why I moved. I got tired of that if you want to see the children then see them and not me."

STEVE: "Can we get a room for a few hours?"

CMO: "Hell No! No more. This pussy is on lockdown when it comes to you and Patience's dad. You won't ever taste these juices again."

Steve continued to talk about having sex with Cmo and she continued to stick to her guns. This was something that she was never able to do before leaving this town, and she would fall into their trap of deception to please him and her other ex-husband in order for her children to see their fathers. He became angry with the answers he was receiving from Cmo.

He began to say that they could only stay for a week. He thought Cmo was staying for at least a week. He knew she was stable with her job and was able to take off for a vacation; that was what he thought she would do. He had made plans for Cmo and him not him and the children. Cmo continued the conversation with the understanding that intercourse in any fashion would never come into existence again.

Cmo left with hope that all would be fine with her children, Steve, and his new family. She was proud of herself; she did not fall into the trap that Steve tried to devise. This angered Steve, but he didn't tell her that, and he definitely didn't show it before she left. Cmo made sure to call daily, checking on the children and sending care packages for each of the three weeks they were there.

Cmo called twice a week to check on the girls, to ensure that the care packages made it and to check and see if the girls needed anything specific for the next shipment; she always spoke with the wife. A week before it was time for the girls to come home, Cmo called and asked for Steve to check for the date and time of their arrival. Steve, even though he was married with a family; told Cmo that since she didn't have sex with him he would not be bringing the girls home.

CMO: "Excuse me..."

STEVE: "I am not bringing the girls home."

CMO: "What?"

STEVE: "I am not bringing the girls home."

CMO: "Steve you don't want to play these games. Not with my children."

STEVE: "I am not bringing the girls home, if you want them then YOU come and get them."

CMO: "Fool! No you are not going to do this. The divorce decree clearly states that you are supposed to bring them to me."

STEVE: "If you want them, come and get them! You should have stayed like I told you too."

CMO: "Stayed? What do you mean?"

By now Cmo was getting pissed off, she could feel her body growing hot with anger.

CMO: "What? Stay and fuck you? Is that why you are doing this? You crazy ass bitch, I'm coming but when I do, you will recognize who you are dealing with. I will make sure of that."

STEVE: "Whatever!"

CMO: "No one keeps my kids from me. You have just opened up a can of whoop ass on many different levels in so many different ways."

STEVE: "Cmo we can settle this, I'll just let my wife know that we have things we need to take care of dealing with the children and I will come alone. We'll spend time together and that will settle your debt. You owe me; I've had them for almost three weeks."

CMO: "Stupid asshole, Peace is your child and Patience only knows you as her father because you were there with her the first three years of life. She calls you daddy. So you're saying that I should pay you for your time spent with your child. Why don't you try being responsible and get a job and make child support payments to assist with your child needs? You don't need to help me with Patience if you don't want too; she is not your biological child anyway."

STEVE: "I miss you Cmo and you have a pussy like no other. I can't get that from no one but you."

CMO: "I will be there to get my babies before the end of the week."

STEVE: "Don't come to my house."

CMO: "WHAT!!? Steve a lot has and haven't happened in our lives this is not a game you want to play, these are my babies. They are all I have in this world to love…"

STEVE: "Love… that is what I am asking for, for you to make love to me."

CMO: "You are just as sick as William."

STEVE: "I don't have the money to get them home to you."

CMO: "WOW! You knew this when I brought them huh..."

STEVE: "I thought you were staying for a least a week to visit family."

CMO: "You made plans for us instead of the kids, didn't you?"

STEVE: "It has just been so long. I know I messed up and I want you back. I was hoping we could just sex it up while you were here."

CMO: "And what about your wife? What does she have to say about all of this?"

STEVE: "It was just for the week I thought you would be here."

CMO: "You are mentally unstable I am coming to get my babies. I don't want no shit when I come either."

STEVE: "OK, tell me this, why you won't have sex with me anymore?"

CMO: "Why should I?"

STEVE: "I miss you and I want to make it up to you."

CMO: "With sex?"

STEVE: "Yes, it's a start."

CMO: "What about the children?"

STEVE: "They are fine they are with you."

CMO: "Right, this is why I am coming to get them at the end of the week with officers if it takes that."

STEVE: "Don't come to my house, you can't have them back!"

Steve knew how Cmo felt about the girls so he only said this to make her bend to his demands.

CMO: "OK, I will be there sooner than you can imagine."

STEVE: "Oh yeah? Humph… Sounds like a threat to me?"

CMO: "A threat?! No it's not a threat or a promise, IT'S A GUARANTEE! Hand delivered and sealed with closed legs and a dry pussy; you don't want what I have to give you. Don't make me have to take it there, please don't."

STEVE: "Well take this then, they will never see you again!"

That was the last thing Steve said to her before he hung up; and Cmo was furious. He'd threaten to take away the two most important people in her life, and on top of that he challenged her. Steve didn't know it yet but he had just written a check that his ass couldn't cash.

Chapter 13

Cmo Gets Her Children Back

Cmo became afraid inside as she planned the trip to get her babies. Cmo would call but Steve and his wife stopped answering the phone. Her feelings and thoughts began to take over as she drove from Chicago, Illinois to Cameron, Pennsylvania. The whole way there she couldn't help but think: *That's how sorry some men are, they can't even uphold their obligations. He was staying with another woman and taking care of her children like they were his. I don't understand how he could love someone else's children more than his own. He couldn't even take responsibility for his own child unless he felt like I would pay him back with sex. He's never there for holidays, he has missed all birthdays. He doesn't even know his child's favorite color the simplest things he never took the time to seek out in regards to his child. Why should I feel like I'm being a whore, sleeping with my ex's just to get him/them to own up to their responsibilities for their child/children? I was prostituting myself for my kids. Now I'm abusing myself so that my girls could see their daddies. I'm worth more than that, I shouldn't have to belittle myself, and by doing that I was shutting down my own self-esteem.*

Cmo would do anything for her children, but she now realized that she needed to stand up for herself. She was hurting herself and this was not going to happen anymore! But when she totally cut it off, even the once or twice a year phone calls from their fathers stopped coming. She never again wanted to feel like a whore for her ex-husbands anymore. She wasn't going to prostitute herself for her children ever again. No one should ever feel so desperate to have to prostitute themselves to have basic needs met for their children or themselves.

If you are in this situation right now, STOP! At one point you may have thought that it would [somehow] become possible for you and your ex to regain a loving and family oriented relationship. Even with all the bad things that are in the past and those bad things that may come with the relationship; you sometimes hoped he or she would come back to you. Thoughts of resuming a bad relationship with thoughts of causing pain to him or her would be wrong for you and wrong to them by all means. Two wrongs don't make a right. There are places to find help for yourself and your children while maintaining your dignity and self-worth.

Cmo, still thinking: *I can't sit around waiting for someone to do something when I know in my heart that it will never happen. I'm not going to lie to myself or others, it is hard. Being a single mother is one of the hardest yet most fulfilling rolls to have in this world. I've made a lot of mistakes along the way because I didn't have anyone to teach me of the things that I should and shouldn't do. I wish there was someone I could have turned to, but I didn't have anyone in my family that I felt I could go to for help. I was so fiercely independent that I didn't want any of them to help me.*

Cmo's family lifestyle hurt her in such a way that it damaged her confidence in them. She didn't want to give the individuals who hurt her in the past an ounce of opportunity to hurt her or her daughters ever again. Cmo declared to build herself up in the arena of independence to show her children that she [alone] could raise them with love as her guide.

Chapter 14

Cmo Becomes Abusive

Life changed in many ways for Cmo, even though a plethora of life lessons were yet to be learned. However, in these transactions of development and growth, Cmo began to become lonely. Cmo had her own apartment and responsibilities, but she began to go out often and wasn't taking care of the girls like a mother should.

A form of depression had taken over. She began to have her children, now seven and ten, taking care of her (sounds familiar?). Cmo hadn't realized that she [in many ways] had become her mother. She was neglecting and abusing her children (remember in the past Cmo swore she would never neglect and abuse her babies). Things seemed to be getting better for Cmo and she began enjoying her new life in Illinois. This was a new start for her and her children but she wasn't treating her children right.

Cmo, as a young lady in her 20's, never had the opportunity to go out and mingle with others. The time had come, one day she decided to have a few people over to her house and they were playing cards and dominoes, drinking, getting high, and shooting the bull. They played all night, and when she woke up the next morning her kitchen was a mess. She and her friends had, literally, trashed the apartment. It was Peace's week to wash dishes. Cmo went into the girls' room to wake up Peace, her youngest daughter.

CMO: "Peace, get up and get the kitchen clean."

PEACE: "Ok mom."

CMO: "Get in there and wash all those dishes now little girl!"

Understand, these were left by Cmo and her drunken friends the night before. Peace got up and found the kitchen looking like someone had just trashed the place and every dish in the house was dirty, so Peace became angry.

PEACE: "Why do I have to clean this kitchen? I didn't dirty it up."

CMO: "Excuse me did you say something?"

PEACE: "No ma'am."

CMO: "You had better straighten up your face little girl..."

PEACE: "Ma'am..."

CMO: "Don't you slam another thing on that cabinet."

PEACE: "Mom I am not doing anything..."

CMO: "You talking back?"

PEACE: "No ma'am..."

CMO: "Girl I will whoop your ass, you better get it done and I mean RIGHT NOW!"

Peace started crying because her feelings were hurt from what her mother was saying. She felt like Cmo had begun to blame her for the mess that she and her friends caused. Peace's older sister walked in to see her little sister crying and asked...

PATIENCE: "Are you ok Peace?"

Peace looked up with tears in her eyes and said...

PEACE: "Mom is making me clean this nasty kitchen that her and her crazy friends messed up. They made this mess last night, why do I have to clean it up? I wish I could leave."

CMO: "I hear everything you saying girl; you gone get the hell knocked out of you for talking back. So stop... Please!"

PATIENCE: "Mom she not talking back."

CMO: "Go to your room Patience, now!"

Patience leaves and now Cmo was angry because she heard every word the girls spoke, and then Peace got bold in her stance, and said…

PEACE: "I want my daddy; I don't want to stay with you anymore."

This angered Cmo. Cmo, not thinking clearly, picked up her child, now seven years old, and threw her across the room. After this action had taken place; it scared the hell out of Cmo.

What have I done?! What have I become?! Oh my God I hurt my child Cmo's mind was racing a mile a minute.

Cmo, at that point, realized who she had become. Finding out that, she too, had an abusive and violent nature. These feelings existed inside of her and have been suppressed for years. Cmo left her daughter on the floor with a nose bleed and ran out of the house to a park about five blocks away. She was afraid that she was going to hurt her child as her mother did to her in the past. Cmo began to fight herself from the grip of her past angers.

Cmo began thinking to herself; *I cannot let this happen but I don't know how to stop it.* This was a familiar anger but Cmo wanted a different outcome. She didn't want to hurt her child in the form of hitting her, because of her anger. What infuriated her the most was the fact that the child stated that she wanted her dad. This is the same dad that she didn't know, one who never paid child support, one who only wanted to see them with Cmo making payments of sex, a man who NEVER called etc… Cmo needed help, so she called a friend, and her friend came over right away. Cmo's nickname in Chicago was Snow. The conversation went like this…

SNOW: "I have done something so wrong; they may take my kids away from me!"

FRIEND: "What Snow? What have you done?"

SNOW: "I threw Peace across the room..."

FRIEND: "What?? Why?!"

SNOW: "The kitchen was dirty after y'all left last night and I woke her up this morning to clean it. Then she had the nerve to say "I want my daddy. I don't want to stay with you no more." I flipped, that ass hole has not been here how can she ever fix her mouth to say those words to me after all I have done?"

FRIEND: "Snow, you need to get some help girl. For some reason you are starting to flip out, are you doing drugs or something?"

The friend began talking to Cmo and trying to speak some sense into her. But all that Cmo could do was cry.

FRIEND: "Calm down you need to get back to the house and make sure she's OK."

SNOW: "She's going to hate me."

FRIEND: "No, she's not... that child loves you. You should have had us clean before we left."

SNOW: "Right, right. OK, I will go back to the house."

On her walk home she began to think of the situation. After getting home, she looked into the eyes of her children, and she begged Peace and Patience for forgiveness. Never had she wanted her children to feel the brunt of her anger.

PEACE: "Mom I'm fine. Are you?"

CMO: "No, I am not fine... I should have NEVER gotten that angry with both of you."

Cmo asked for God's forgiveness, but it still hurt her so badly. She felt the pain that she caused her child. But through it all, Peace yet loved her momma. Peace forgave her mother for the abuse which made Cmo take notice and she began to make changes in their lives.

If you ever feel you're getting to that point where you're not sure if you might hurt your child or yourself, please call for help. Fear and anger should not lead you to be violent. Children should have the freedom of speech around you [as parents] with respect. We should want them to tell us what they need and what they are feeling at all times because in Cmo's case, she didn't have it around her while she was growing up. But, even though they have freedom of speech, they should always remember who the adults are. A parent must lead by example and be firm in love.

Cmo wasn't allowed to have an opinion, so that should have triggered her to act differently with her children. But, we as parents have and opinion and that opinion may not always work, parenting does not come with a manual. Cmo felt as though her mother should have, at least, listened to her, but she didn't. Cmo wanted her home to be a safe place where her children could be honest with themselves and with her. Cmo made and will make mistakes, but at least she is trying to correct some of the errors made by her mom.

Chapter 15

Patience and Peace

Patience and Peace loved each other very much; they were like two peas in a pod. Peace wasn't only Patience's' sister, Peace became Patience's baby. They began to learn that having each other was the first step to having love within the family. They were each other's keeper and they protected each other, no matter what.

Patience was one of those children, whom felt, she had to do it all and know it all. It was all about her at times, but she did take good care of her little sister. Patience became very protective of her sister, she was in High School and Peace was in Middle School. Patience would sometimes skip school to tend to her sister's needs. Cmo went to work, daily, worrying about her child's behavior. Cmo began to ask different organizations about mentors, but places [such as those in Cmo's eyes]were not safe. Cmo was very protective when it came to her children. In the presence of others, Cmo's children were perfect and no one could convince her otherwise. She would be ready to fight; even if they were wrong she was one to whoop your ass if you disrespected them. Anyways, Cmo heard how some of these places may be abusive in different ways. She heard that many children may have gotten abused by their mentors, foster parents, guardians, grandparents, and a host of other different people whom they loved and trusted.

Cmo would kill if she ever thought her children were being abused by the hands or mouth of another. Cmo became paranoid as to the protection and care of her children. She would not let just anyone keep her children. She never wanted to get rid of her children. She woke up to her children, she lived for her children, she wanted to be the best mom in the World for her children; working daily showing them love from herself and their missing fathers.

To sum it all up, Cmo was a lunatic when it came to her children. Nevertheless, she would worry about Patience getting in trouble, because she knew they may send her to prison if her daughter ran across the wrong person. She would worry about the police stopping her and giving her tickets and her finding out later. Patience was the kind of person...well; let's just say that she was just like her momma. She had to see it for herself, know it for herself and do it for herself. So Cmo had to be very careful with her baby, because of their likeness. That's what Cmo's mother never figured out in her years many of parenting. Cmo rectified this by giving her children freedom to speak aloud but with respect.

Cmo children were able to talk to her and tell her how they felt about anything and everything. The topic of the conversation didn't matter; she would speak about different issues of life. When Cmo's children would ask her questions and she didn't know the answer; you better believe that she would eventually get an answer for those questions.

Not all parents feel comfortable doing this, they don't feel like they have the answers and don't want to be embarrassed. If you do not feel comfortable talking to your children about a topic, find someone you trust to be there for them to answer these types of questions. It can be another family member, someone at church, or at their school. Just make sure that the person stepping in and advising them is telling it how you'd want to tell it. This is where Cmo had issues because she didn't want anyone speaking to her children.

One day Patience, now fifteen, decided she wanted to steal from her mother. She would take her mother's pager or cell phone to school and would lie about it. Now mind you, this is a child that's been skipping school, has gotten a ticket, and had to do forty hours of community service for her actions. Despite all of that, she was not a problem child.

She was just a behaviorally dysfunctional child in regards to her behavior right now. Unbeknownst to Cmo, Patience was still missing her dad in her life and she thought her mother was confused and life seemed unfair to her. She grew up following her peers, but it wasn't their fault. Patience had her own agenda and Cmo couldn't blame anyone else for what her child was doing and going through. Patience began seeing her friends getting into trouble, and being disobedient. Cmo would quote to Patience…

CMO: "Patience, if you see other people doing wrong, it doesn't mean you've got to do it too… You have followers and you have leaders; be a leader and make a difference."

This particular time when Patience lied and stole from her mother, Cmo would not over-look it. Cmo confronted her about the lying and stealing. Patience started getting loud with her mom. Cmo told her that she had had enough and she would be punished for her crimes of lying and stealing. Cmo was going to whoop her when they got home and she did, she whooped her child. Now [while whooping her child] Patience raised her hand to her mother. Cmo was shocked she began thinking, *What the hell? I just know this little girl is not trying to jump into a grown woman role; I am her mama...*

CMO: "What? You gone raise your hand and hit me!? Oh, no, did you forget?"

PATIENCE: "Forget what?"

Cmo lost it; she instantly became another person to her child. Mother stepped aside and this wild woman commenced whopping her child. She was totally wrong, believe it, she was wrong for what she did because she lost control of her anger.

Understand this, we as parents will lose it sometimes. It's not wrong to discipline a child, but it is wrong to lose control. That's when discipline became abuse. If you cannot control yourself when you get angry then you need to get some help before your child gets seriously hurt. Being a full-time parent, especially if you are a single parent, is scary. It's more than a full time job, there is so much responsibility and it can be overwhelming. But then again, there are people out there who can show you how to discipline your child without losing control. There wasn't any viable excuse for her child to be raising her hand to her, but Cmo went overboard. She, as a mother, was wrong.

After the beating, Peace and Cmo went to the store and while they were there, Cmo got a phone call. It was the Police Department.

OFFICER: "We're at your apartment waiting for you to come home."

CMO: "Did my daughter call the police on me?"

OFFICER: "Yes, ma'am, she did. We understand that there was an incident that happened in this house."

CMO: "I'll tell you what... I'll be there in five minutes to talk to you about this just hold on."

This officer was in her house and you know what she did? She walked in and said...

CMO: "You need to handcuff me now."

OFFICER: "Ma'am, we just want to talk to you."

CMO: "No, you need to handcuff me because when y'all leave I'm whopping that as again. The fact of the matter is that I'm her mother (turning to her child) and you're going to call the police on me when you're the one in the wrong. Yeah, I went overboard, and I'm saying this in front of the police. I may have gone a bit much on the overboard side, but she not bruised or anything. The only thing hurting are her feelings. I'm trying to take care of my household so that my child won't be out on the street doing something wrong and end up getting shot or arrested. I'm trying to train her right and she's steering of in the wrong direction. I'm going to do my best to see that my children are trained right at home, but what they do outside, they are going to do on their own and I can't control that."

OFFICER: "Ma'am, we're going to send Child Protective Services out here to talk to you anyway."

CMO: "Well, you do that, but in the meantime I'm going to acknowledge my wrong, and I'm going to have to take care of me and my family and in taking care of me and my family I need to get us some help. I see now that I have a serious anger problem. I can't blame this anger problem on no one else, it is all me. It isn't 'monkey see, monkey do' anymore; it is me in need of assistance."

The Child Protective Services (CPS) lady came over and said.

CPS LADY: "What can we do to help you?"

CMO: "You can't do anything for me, not today. This is Friday, so just give me until Monday and I'll find me and my family some help; I don't need you to help me. I'll call you Monday and inform you of the help we've gotten."

CPS LADY: "OK, but you do understand that we will need to take action on this case if it is found that you are a potential threat to your children?"

CMO: "Yes, ma'am I do understand but it is me and I will get the help needed for my family. Thank you."

When the CPS Lady left, Cmo began searching for a class that could assist them and found a place called Behavioral Home for Children in the same state, but it was 400 miles from her home. After speaking to a care consultant, Cmo decided that it was the best process for her, her daughter, and their family. So, she decided to send Patience away for a year to get her the help she needed.

In the meantime the CPS Lady called…

CPS LADY: "Hello, I would like to make an appointment with you concerning the children."

CMO: "OK, what is it you want to know?"

CPS LADY: "How are they?"

CMO: "They are fine; Patience is in Behavioral School in another city."

CPS LADY: "Really?"

CMO: "Yes really, they give the parents counseling and they give the children counseling. They teach the kids how to deal with their anger, their feelings, their lying, their cheating, and their mischievousness. It, also, teaches them how to deal with themselves and how to take responsibilities for their actions. Meanwhile, the whole family will have counseling and we will all have family therapy."

Cmo's baby went to this behavioral school and learned very well. In this process Cmo and her children began to get along better. They both understood that they had issues. They learned how to take care of themselves, their problems, and the understanding of their surroundings. They also learned how to work with anger and how to [not] let everything trigger it within them. Learning how to walk away from it, deal with it,and how to come back and let it be communicated in the proper manner.

The people at the Behavioral Home for Children were wonderful to her and her family. They were able to learn the values of self through training on how to motivate without anger or pressure. Cmo found out that she had some real serious issues deriving from her past developments and family history that she had never forgiven and gotten over. This was the greatest help Cmo could have ever gotten. In saving the integrity of her family as a whole; the family structure became a valuable gift of love to Cmo. She finally understood the whole concept of family a foundation.

Patience went on to graduate at a private school after that. Now some people tell their children, "If you ever get pregnant I'll put you out, you're going to be on your own, I will kill you, you won't have it, etc." But Cmo never said those things to her children. Although she did not want them to get pregnant, she did feel that because of their open relationship, she had it under control. She would often say…

CMO: "Don't get pregnant while you are young. Look at me; let me be the example of getting pregnant at a young and naïve stage in your life, learn from my mistakes."

However, one day as they were at the car care center (Cmo was getting her oil changed) Patience, now seventeen years old, said…

PATIENCE: "Mom I need to tell you something."

CMO: "What's that, honey?"

PATIENCE: "I'm pregnant."

    Cmo stood up and began walking towards her, but Patience started backing up. Patience thought Cmo was going to hit her, but instead Cmo said…

CMO: "Come here."

PATIENCE: "No mom, you're going to hit me."

CMO: "I'm not going to hit you child. Come here… Come here baby."

Peace said to her sister…

PEACE: "Go! Start running!"

    But Patience walked over to her mom. Cmo took her baby by the hand, put her arms around her and hugged her and said…

CMO: "We'll work this out. It's going to be all right, baby, this is something that we're going to work out together."

It is all in the approach to your child. This is the reaction Cmo would have loved to have received from her mother; nevertheless, Cmo made it through her mother's harsh language, abuse and neglect after her mother found out that she was pregnant. Cmo's mom put her out of their home.

Parents don't tell your children you're going to kill them, beat them or put them out if they get pregnant. Don't beat them down, but love them up. That is what they need, they are scared and feeling lost. They need someone to help them sort through their different options. Patience's, being pregnant, was a huge shock and a great un-expectancy in their lives as a whole. Cmo was in shock but put off her guilt and pain to comfort her child. I mentioned guilt, yes guilt because we all have that question of "What have I done to cause this?". Well understand this; most of you will get upset with this statement, but this is real talk... You are raising your children to the best of your ability, this child made a grown-up decision which resulted in a grown-up consequence. Cmo, as the mother, was nowhere around when this action took place. So stop blaming yourselves as parents for the choices your child makes. Yes, we are the supporters and the value-setters for the family but [in the end] your child has free will to do what they want. It is up to them whether to take heed to your instruction, or not.

Patience ended up having a hard time carrying the baby, just like her mother did when she was pregnant with her children. Cmo became passionate because she knew of the fear of caring a child. There was a great possibility that Patience would lose her baby. Cmo had to be there for Patience because she knew the pain associated with the loss of a child and she did not want this for her child. Cmo understood that this was a case of a child carrying a child. Even though Patience now had the responsibility of caring for her child, she was so scared, but her mother never failed her. Cmo had always been there for her children. When the baby was born he was a sick, but he made it through that sickness and now he's the man of the house. Though they were not able to teach him all the manly things, they found out that they could teach him how they, as women, want to be treated by a man. They began teaching him how to be the little boy that respects, in hopes that one day he would grow into a great young man.

Put yourself in their place. Remember your time of growth, what is your story? We have all fallen short of our moral values and we have all been punished and most of us with the concept of love punish ourselves more often than others. We are harder on self than others can ever be.

Chapter 16

A Night Out

Cmo's life began to feel as if she was doing all that it took to be a good mother without any sort of freedom to go out and have a little fun. She had a good job, there was a roof over their heads, food on the table, and money in their pocket [however] something was missing. Cmo was lonely... so, eventually, she began to date. One night she prepared to go out to happy hour with her co-workers, she lived downtown and only two blocks from the bar. She arrived around 7pm, and sometime between 7pm and 10 pm, she drank two Climax cocktails. It was a great night of fun and relaxation for Cmo. Around 10:30 pm, she and her co-workers decided it was time to leave the bar.

CMO: "My treat!"

HER GROUP: "Wow, really Ok, Ok, on me next time…"

She took out her card and handed it to the bartender. The bar became very crowded and noisy. A young man asked her to dance and she accepted. When she got up to dance she yelled to one of her co-workers...

CMO: "Get my card when she comes back!!!"

CO-WORKER: "OK!!!"

She started dancing and enjoying herself. They had a short conversation and introduce themselves and after two songs have played she decided to go back to her seat. But her co-worker was up dancing so now she was the one sitting down and waiting. Paul (the young man she was dancing with) came back and asked her for her phone number.

CMO: "Sorry I don't know you well enough to give you my number."

PAUL: "Ok that's fine but how will I get to know you if we don't call each other though?"

CMO: "How often do you come here?"

PAUL: "Pretty often..."

CMO: "Well Ok. Will you be here next Friday night?"

PAUL: "Yes I will..."

PAUL: "Good, then I will come next Friday."

PAUL: "Are you sure?"

CMO: "Yes."

PAUL: "Great, it's a date."

Her co-worker approached the table and said,

CO-WORKER: "The rest of them are staying here but I'm ready to go are you ready girl...?"

CMO: "Yes I am, how about we make this our spot after work on next Friday?"

CO-WORKER: "Girl yeah, I am having so much fun. I haven't done this in a while."

Cmo turned to Paul and remembering what he said about a date said...

CMO: "No, not a date we will just meet and have drinks. I will be with my co-worker again."

PAUL: "Ok see you then."

Not focusing on their surroundings, Cmo and her co-worker began to converse again, her co-worker said...

CO-WORKER: "Don't you just live two blocks down the street."

CMO: "Yes I do."

CO-WORKER: "I will drop you off; this way we both will be safe, me walking to my car and you getting home."

CMO: "Alright. That's cool..."

Paul was still standing there listening to their whole conversation.

PAUL: "I'll walk you home since it's that close."

CMO: "What? Oh...No. That's Ok I will ride with my co-worker..."

PAUL: "Ok, let me get out of here too... see you Friday...?"

CMO: "Alright..."

Cmo and her co-worker walked to the car, still conversing about the events of the night.

CO-WORKER: "So what you think?"

CMO: "About what?"

CO-WORKER: "About the bar, you've never been to a Chicago bar before. Did you like it; was it fun?"

CMO: "Oh, wow I had a great time. Let's make sure we go next week."

CO-WORKER: "Oh my, Why?"

CMO: "I had such a great time,I just want to do it again."

Coworker: "Ok now that we're on the subject of coming next week. Should I bring someone with me?"

CMO: "Why?"

CO-WORKER: "You're going to be with that guy, right…"

CMO: "Sort of, he was kind of cute…"

CO-WORKER: "Ok"

Getting in the car Cmo looked up and saw Paul walking to his car.

CMO: "Damn he looks good..."

They laugh and with finishing up their conversation about the night, Cmo got out of the car and said....

CMO: "Oh, give me my card?"

CO-WORKER: "Damn, I forgot to get it... I'm sorry girl.'

CMO: "That's cool, I'll just go back and get it."

Her co-worker thought that Cmo would get in her car and drive over there, so she pulled off and waved good-bye. But after considering the time it would take get the car, Cmo decided to walk. As she was walking back to the bar, she sees Paul in his car. Then Paul noticed Cmo and makes a U-turn and waved her down.

PAUL: "Want a ride."

CMO: "No that's OK, I'm just going back to get my card."

Guy: "You sure?"

CMO: "Yes I am thank you."

PAUL: "Ok."

He drove off as she reached the bar. Cmo ended up being at the bar for an extra 20 or 30 minutes getting her card. She was so frustrated, so she made sure to calm herself down while walking home. Someone in a 1980's Lincoln Town Car interrupted her thoughts by asking for directions. She said nothing and continued to walk, quickening her pace.

But, he continued driving beside her, slowly, and then came to a complete stop. Cmo was on the curb waiting for the light to change before crossing the street. In fear, while the light was still red, she began crossing the street. The car screeched away, made a U-turn, ran the red light and stopped in front of her. The rear door opened and up pops Paul, the guy that she danced with. She began to run. She was only a block away from home, but then Paul started chasing her. She made it to her building but Paul grabbed her and threw her into the car, all the while she was screaming and no one came to help her.

DRIVER: "Shut the fuck up!"

PAUL: "We're not going to hurt you we just want to have a little fun."

CMO: "Why me, you had so many other choice, why me…"

PAUL: "No we were waiting for you."

CMO: "Waiting for me?"

PAUL: "We just wanted to fuck around."

CMO: "What? No, I need to get home."

The driver became silent, but Paul began to ask what would be the charge for a little fun.

PAUL: "Can we go to your place."

CMO: "No my sisters are home. (When in actuality it would be her 18 year old, her grandbaby and her youngest daughter who was 15 at the time)"

Cmo made this statement because she knew her babies were home and she just didn't know her kidnappers plan. They drove to a cheap motel; it was a place that you would pay for by the hour. They escorted her into the bedroom and told her to sit on the bed and undress. Cmo started crying looking at the two men before her; she pictured in her mind that they were just two terrifying Williams' (ex-husband). She began to remember the horrific things that William did to her, playing back the years of abuse in her mind. She had been raped so much by William, she didn't want that feeling anymore so she began to think; *I will show them the time of their lives; they will be begging for more.*

All at once, her feelings of anxiety and hopelessness turned into conning and mischievous. So she began to play alone and she became another person 'STORM'. Her alter ego, Storm, was a prostitute who actually raped her capturers. She was a wave of explosions with a tornado sprit. Revulsion became her typhoon, riveting became her downpour, detestation became her rainstorm, resentment was her blizzard, distaste became her hurricane, rage became her foot stool, and the power to hurt and destroy the male being became endemic. This was the night that Cmo became "STORM". With an innocent movement, intended to tease, she turned towards Paul, moving seductively slow, rubbed her breast slightly against his chest and said.

STORM: "Now that we are here what would you like?"

PAUL: "OH, so now you gon act right?"

STORM: "Shit I might as well, we are here and I do want a touch of what you have."

PAUL: "What do you mean?"

SECOND GUY: "WOW! It looks like she wants to fuck".

STORM: "No I don't want to fuck…"

SECOND GUY: "Well what?"

STORM: "I want to be the bun for both of you; my buns are hot and ready."

PAUL: "OK, let's do this."

Storm laid on the bed and opened her legs and said…

STORM: "Look what do you see?"

Both guys were in suspense as to what Storm doing. She was giving them a show to remember by setting the atmosphere with anticipation and expectation of them having the time of their lives. Storm looked at the men pants to see that they were fully erected, that was exactly what she wanted. She then unbuckled Paul's pants, Paul was standing in shock as she began to put her mouth on him; but all at once she stopped. She thought about

William, so she spit in her hands and began to rub on Paul at the same time summoning for the second guy to come over and take his pants off too. While the second guy took off his paints she grabbed his penis and began to stoke it in the same motion as she was stroking Paul's penis.

STORM: "You guys feeling as strong and hard as your dicks are?"

BOTH: "Damn you are good."

Now these guys don't know of Cmo's past history of abuse and neglect, they also didn't know that they just become victims of 'STORM'. She then informed the guys that she wanted to play a role with them.

PAUL: "You're a freak huh?"

STORM: "More than you know..."

SECOND GUY: "What role do you want me to play?"

These guys had forgotten that they were once in charge but the tables had turned, and now Storm was the dictator.

STORM: "I want Paul to be in position for the top (pussy) and you for the bottom (butt)."

Neither of you can touch me with your hands, but you must insert your dicks inside of me. The first one who can get it in will get the fuck of a life time.

SECOND GUY: "What if we both get it in?"

STORM: "Two dicks at the same time is a treat for us all."

PAUL: "Well fuck let's do it."

These guys were enjoying the sensuous rub down, they were into the act so they both exclaimed that they wanted her to stop and let them put it in. But Storm just continued, acting like she didn't hear them but the intenseness of her movements just made the men more vulnerable. She began to talk to them because she saw that the eruption was about to take place.

STORM: "I see the volcano is about to explode."

SECOND GUY: "NO, no, no, not now, stop!"

But it's too late; they simultaneously let go of their foul nectar. But Cmo did not stop, she made a movement with her breast while her bra was still on, she slid one of the dicks between her breast (nice and tight between her bra) while both dicks were covered with their nectar; now flowing on her breast. Paul, not being able to take this sensation, unsnapped her bra completely off and this too turned the guys on and again they release their foul nectar. Seeing the shine of the nectar on her breast as she rubbed it in...

STORM: "How do you guys feel now?"

PAUL: "WOW, lady I have never had that done? What was that?"

STORM: "That was sex outside the vagina without penetration."

SECOND GUY: "What?"

STORM: "Yes that's a little something my ex-husband taught me when I was with him."

PAUL: "I know he would kill for that pussy?"

STORM: "How would you know, you never had it?"

PAUL: "SHIT!! You're this good with your hands; no doubt you can make that pussy go 'clap, clap'?"

STORM: "Yes I can and I can also make my ass clamp a tight grip on that dick too."

She noticed that the men were aroused again. Now understand Storm's motive is to not get penetrated by either of her abusers (did you forget these are her abusers even though she has turned the tables, she is still in danger) she was doing all this talking and playing because she did not want them to actually insert their penises into her. She now asked them to sit on the bed and she began to give them both lap dances and this also caused them both to ejaculate.

STORM: "Do either of you have a fantasy maybe we can do it now."

PAUL: "I have one?"

STORM: "What is it?"

SECOND GUY: "I want to fuck you and see what's between your legs."

PAUL: "Yeah me too... that shit has to be hot as hell."

STORM: "You want "hot as hell" I'll give you a feel but you both have to go and wash your hands very well?"

PAUL: "What?"

STORM: "Just do it. OK?"

They each go to the bathroom and when they are done. They found Storm lying on the bed naked.

You probably thought that she would have left, but no, the mission was not done. The guys were shocked, but to their disadvantage, they were not hard anymore.

STORM: "I see I have to work again? For this I will need for you to give me something?"

PAUL: "What? What's your cost?"

STORM: "$200.00"

SECOND GUY: "OK, I have it right here."

Storm put the money into her ass for safe keeping but that amazed the guys. She then slid her fingers into herself and when she took her fingers out she showed them her nectar. Paul was aroused and the second guy was pounding away at his own dick. Paul moved in closer and Storm said…

STORM: "Can you see it?"

PAUL: "What? WOW you look like you are swelling?"

STORM: "I'm going to come you need to move…"

PAUL: "No I want to see…"

STORM: "I am a squirter, you need to move Now!!"

BOTH: "OH SHIT!!"

STORM: "OH! I am going to give you your monies worth."

BOTH: "DAMN, WOW! What the fuck was that?"

STORM: "That is a squirter."

Both men were in shock but just as quickly as it started it was over and they both felt satisfied. Storm had completed her mission and now Cmo was ready to go, she began putting on her clothes in anticipation of getting the hell up out of there.

PAUL: "When can I see you again?"

CMO: "We will talk about, I'll give you both my number. But I must get home before my sisters call the cops."

PAUL: "Yeah, you're right we will take you home."

CMO: "OK."

Cmo had the men drop her off at another building where she pretended to stay. As soon as they were out of sight, Cmo ran home as fast as she could, making sure to look over her shoulders. When Cmo got home she found her girls up watching movies and she asked them how their night was as if nothing had happened to her.

CMO: "Ya'll are up mighty late, what's wrong?"

PATIENCE: "Little man (the baby) had a rough night. He just fell asleep."

CMO: "Is he Ok now?"

PATIENCE: "Yes ma'am."

PEACE: "How was your night? You look exhausted?"

CMO: "I'm good baby. I had fun, but I am ready to take a shower and get in my bed. Oh, I have something for the both of you bu,t you must share with the baby. okay?"

BOTH GIRLS: "Okay, mom."

CMO: "Okay, I will give it to you all tomorrow."

BOTH GIRLS: "Okay Mom, goodnight..."

CMO: "Night girls."

She closed the door and began to reflect back on the events of the night and with those thoughts, she cried. She became saddened by her actions with her captures, but his was her only means of survival. Had she not been the thoughtful one in the situation she may have ended up dead along with her children. She decided instead of fighting back and angering her abusers, to surrender and possibly save her life and the life of her family.

This is not something I would recommend for anyone, but this was the process that worked for Cmo at the time.

The next day the girls got up and went into Cmo's room only to discover their mother was crying, with swollen eyes she said...

CMO: "I love you guys, I want to let you both know... something happened to me last night."

BOTH GIRLS: "Mom what's wrong?"

CMO: "Sometimes you get caught up in the wrong things and life takes a turn for the worst, andthe decision you make can hurt you."

PEACE: "What's wrong mom?"

PATIENCE: "Are you hurt mom?"

CMO: "Yes, yes love (crying) I am very hurt because of my life. I have been raped in a way; you both may not understand what I mean right now but, I am beginning to see what my mother has said for years. Patience, Peace your mom has been wronged and I have wronged."

She began telling them a clean version of the night before, but yet painting a picture of her pain, so that her girls would be watchful in all they did. Cmo would always explain to her children the good, bad, and indifferent so that they too would have an image of the rights and wrongs. They talked about many things the conversation began with Cmo saying…

CMO: "Please forgive me. I have been a mother in despair. Not knowing how to raise you girls, I blamed it all on my mother, but I can no longer blame her for my decisions. I have finally realized my own faults. I was a rebellious, spoiled, mischievous, and inconsiderate child all my life looking for what I already had, just not knowing how to grab it and embrace it. If I had taken the time to listen instead of just stepping out on the unknown I may have had a relationship with my mom."

The girls understood their mother's cry and forgave her and they began to talk about issues as if they stepped into a conference on abuse, neglect, and shame. This conversation led to a conversation of love building and while in this conversation Cmo began to cry even the more.

PATIENCE: "Mom what's wrong now?"

CMO: "I miss my mom..."

The girls both looked at each other as to say "What?' This had never [ever] come out of Cmo's mouth before.

PEACE: "Mom if she ever comes around, how are we to treat her?"

CMO: "Baby, love her, always love her. I was treated with the only love she knew this is why I am saying these things to you. My mom loved me with all of her heart and all she wanted was the best for me. It was I that rejected her and caused her and myself pain."

PATIENCE: "Mom I don't understand?'

CMO: "I blamed my mom for all of my wrongs, but how can you blame someone for your own decisions? God has let me know that this is my life and what it is today is what I made it. Once I take responsibility all will work out. Let me give you an example: If I meet the drug man that is my decision. I made the call to meet, I took the time to meet him, I paid for my product, I drove home with my own gas, I open and closed the door to the car both ways, after getting home I set it up and I puffed the pipe on my own. I caused harm to myself. But I would say I hate my mom for my pains. Look we make decisions on a daily basis and we cannot blame another person for our choices. My mom has done her best and I need to appreciate her for the good. I know what is right and wrong because of her and this is why I have grown up overnight. You know how sometimes I look at you girls when you get up; I can see in many ways your growth. That's why sometimes I say "Wow, you grew up overnight.' Well this time mom grew up overnight. I realized who I was and know who I am now. I want you both to forgive me for my lack and I promise I will do better."

BOTH GIRLS: "We love you mom."

CMO: "Group hug."

That night Cmo prayed to God, something she had not done in years. She asked Him "Why am I like this?" She felt that she had, now, been put on notice to do better. Life became a big mess so she moved closer to her hometown where she was born and the children began to be happier. That is when Cmo realized that she truly had become a mother.

Chapter 17

God-given Name

Cmo would tell people all the time that when she was born, her mother named her Cmo Jenkins, but when her babies were born, she received a different name. It was her heavenly name given by God. Her name was Mother. She now understood the name and the role of a Mother. She had been living in fear, trying to figure out how to be a mother.

Yes, it can be scary, but it's something that we must to do. We [as mothers] have a need to do, want to do, should do, and are just going to do for our children no matter what. Cmo would often ask God, "Why did you make me a mother? This responsibility is hard." Being a mother is one of the scariest things a person can do in their life; in my opinion. You are responsible for the lives of another, your baby. To be a mother you've got to do it right. We, as mothers, hear this all the time 'God knows what he's doing.' You know what; I am beginning to believe that from this story alone. These all sound like lessons learned by Cmo this woman has been through so many heartaches and pains [many not mentioned] God has to be with her. God takes care of Cmo and he loosed the shackles in her life. God protected Cmo every step of the way.

Chapter 18

Cmo Finds Herself

Cmo often swore to herself that when she left her mother's home, she would never return. She swore that she would find a way to break the cycle of abuse in her family. But while all these 'Lessons Learned' are taking place, Cmo became the abuser to her mother and all men who crossed her path.

Augustine opened a non-profit organization, helping young women who were victims of abuse (thinking of her child). See, Cmo's mother heard about her wild side. So she took the pain and channeled it into helping others. While Cmo's mother was working Cmo was now living in her hometown but, no one knew. One day Cmo looked in the mirror, and she saw nothing. She was nothing but a lost and broken individual. A person who had not taken responsibility of any of her self-issues, a person who needed loving, a person who needed to learn how to love, a person who wanted her mother in her life, and a person who had become confused. Cmo became "STORM" a person who had many different traits, an abuser of drugs and clubs, and a prostitute.

She was taunting men for many years, and soon, not only were men her captives; but, she went on to become one of the highest paid Madams in 30 States. She recruited men and women, teaching them the sensual points and how to give each of their clients the sensation of a lifetime to keep them coming back for more. In the meantime, she manipulated the mind of the captured. She would teach her members that if they could sensually please (without penetration) without the act of sexual intercourse (penetration) then they would get a bonus. "How sick was that?!"

She felt that if the explosion of a man never entered into the body of the other, it would not be considered a sexual act. But one day, in her moment of despair she realized that she had not only become the misunderstanding of a mother's love, but she had also become her own abuser. Someone her mother would not be proud of. This was the cause of Cmo's rage. Her mother would say many times, "Cmo, if you don't change your ways, your ways will be the death of your mind, body, and soul."

Cmo had something bad to happen to her and her family after moving back to the old neighborhood. She lost Peace to violence. Peace was murdered by the hands of a young man while in high school. Cmo's children were her reasons and means to get up in the mornings. Patience and Peace were the reasons for Cmo's existence. Cmo lived for her children. The children were all she needed; she felt God only needed to wake her up every morning to care for her children; in a manner she thought she never had. Not realizing that her mother Augustine was doing the very same thing, reaching out for love as she matured. However, with her reach of love, the rejection of acceptance is at the forefront. This was because of her firmness and the misunderstanding of self, not knowing how to channel the anger into a positive mode; so that she may prosper from the love given. Cmo, unaware of the type of anger she possessed; became angry daily with the act of sensual teasing and pleasing of men and women.

However, in many ways Cmo became worst; she recruited others into her acts of deception. Cmo, standing looking in the mirror crying, saddened by her loss and longing for Peace; this world was no longer hers; her thoughts were of death and wanting to find the Peace she had lost. She realized that day, that she and her mother were both raising their children without training, both doing the best they knew how, as did her mother and her mother before her. This was a cycle no one sought help for because it had become a familiar way of life for all involved. But Cmo was born with a longing to love while inheriting the abusive behaviors of the family's generational curse. But, Cmo became familiar with the feelings of abuse and neglect. She just wanted to love others as she loved her children.

Now in misery and no peace of mind, Cmo's oldest daughter Patience and her grandson moved out; because of the neglect on Cmo's part. After the loss of Peace, Cmo felt like she should have been the one to die. So her guilt and trying to die silently (suicide) carried her into a world-wind of giving, giving away all she had to others, but nothing to her and her family. She needed to stay busy to forget or get past the pain of the loss of her loved ones, her son and daughter, both lost to abuse and violence.

Cmo now carried her guilt, and this is because she lived and her daughter was killed. See, because of the loss of Peace, Cmo neglected Patience and her grandson. When she lost Peace she gave up on Patience too. Patience was hurt because she needed her mom, but upon the death of Peace Cmo also died within herself. She felt like she would never make things right with Patience because of her sister's death. The guilt of Cmo not dying before her children haunted her for years. Cmo stopped calling her own child and moved into a different direction and this too was a path straight to hell. She came to the realization that her mother was the best mom she could have ever had. It was at that moment that Cmo realized her mother was trying to break a cycle of abuse herself; but didn't know how.

Question: How many of you have grown into your mother?

All of us have, in one way or the other, examined ourselves before. Though you may think that you've turned into your mother, you have a choice somake the best of you. Let your definition of self-esteem, self-motivation and self-appreciation become "LOVE" (Learning Our Value Everyday) because you are worth being loved.

Some folks sit up and they say… "My parents made me do this, and my parents made me do that." Well, parents can be an influence, but who made the decision to actually step out and do it? You did. Cmo made all the decision in her life and actually stepped out and did everything that she did; she had no reason to blame her mother. Her mother taught her the best way she knew how. Cmo's whole problem was that she had to see everything for herself and she thought that being in the Church wouldn't help her. Other people said 'That's demonized.' No, that's just being rebellious and being a child. Cmo didn't want to understand the Church. She felt she wasn't ready for church. So she had issues and she had problems. She would say…

CMO: "Some people who I call 'holier than thou' say you have to walk straight, talk straight, move straight, sit straight, wear your hair straight, and wear long sleeves and long dresses etc... You had to cover up everything. You had to do this and you had to do that according to the minister."

That's her view of the church, but everybody has a right to do things their own way based on their own upbringing. If you don't want to be a part of that, move around and get involved into what suits you. Don't stay in something you don't like. That's a form of abuse because you are letting them control and manipulate you to do what you don't want to do. Like I said before, abuse comes in many different ways. She was abused and she has been the abuser. You must learn how to break those cycles of abuse; and she did, by stepping away.

CMO: "Whatever god they serve, I don't want to have nothing to do with that one, and guess what? I mean that. Whatever god you serve, that keeps you restricted and restrained, I don't want to have anything to do with that god. The one I serve is a forgiving God. He's a loving God. He loves me no matter what I do. He appreciates me for being me because, in return, I appreciate Him for just being Him, an awesome God. Whoever is your higher power, you serve him and you serve him well because I will serve my higher power to the utmost. The reason I serve Him is that He forgives me. He loves me. I'm not going to make anybody or anything bigger than Him."

I don't understand the way people act, not just Cmo's family, this involves everyone in the whole World. Let me give you an example, you are at your house drinking. You have your rum and coke or Seagram seven and you're feeling a little feeling of calmness, because that's what happens to me when I drink. Drinking relaxes me. So there you are at your house and you are drinking and all of a sudden your pastor knocks at the door. It could be a pastor you haven't seen in years, or a missionary, or a deacon, or someone you think is of some kind of authority in your church. What are you going to do, act like you aren't drinking? Spray your breath down, put a mint in, or put some gum in because you don't want that man or that woman to know you were in your house drinking? Better yet, say you are out and you're having dinner and you have a Daiquiri sitting at your table and your minister comes to your table and says, "How are you doing, sister/brother?" What are you going to do with that drink? Are you going to feel guilty because your pastor sees that drink or are you going to feel guilty because he knows you drink? I have news for you. God saw it when you ordered it. Your higher power saw it before you even drank it. Your higher power knew you were going to get it before you even ordered it. So in my book, you have just disrespected your higher power.

You have just disrespected God because you just put a man on earth over the Father in Heaven. Giving man respect by trying to hid the evidence but God sees you. See, that's what people couldn't understand about Cmo. Yes, her mother is a strong member of Church and she respects her Father in Heaven also, she also respects her pastor, but if she is drinking in her house and you come over unannounced don't expect her to stop what she is doing. Don't try to come in her home and put her down, because you came over to her house. Accept her for who she is and pray, let her see your good spirit.

CMO: "Let me see your acceptance of a sinner if that's what you call a sinner, but don't come into my house saying "God don't like that you're drinking" because I already know this and I'm doing it anyway. I don't need to hear it from you. I don't want to hear, "If you do that you're going to go to hell." Now see, that right there, that's the kind of shit the messed me up."

People were always telling her that she was going to hell for doing what she does. Because her family always threw up negative power this is another reason she left them.

CMO: "If I'm going to drink I'm going to drink. If I'm going to smoke, I'm going to smoke. Whatever it is that I do, I'm going to do just that. I'm not going to become someone else just for you. That's allowing you to manipulate me, define me and abuse me by taking control over me. You're not bigger than the God I serve. You're not bigger than the God who wakes me up every day. He sees me put my pants on one leg at a time. He sees me put my makeup on and he sees me put on my earrings. He sees me dye my hair. I can't be fake, and that's why I don't get along with fake people. I wasn't accepted because I wasn't going to stop doing what I was doing. I gave them their respect when they were in my house. I didn't drink anymore until they left, but I wasn't going to pour my drink out and pretend either. Be straight up. Don't play with life."

Sometimes when growing up, different ones may tend to mimic what their parents do because that's the only training they may be receiving at that time. The Bible says "Train up a child in the way he should go: and when he is old, he will not depart from it" (King James Bible *Cambridge Ed.*, Proverbs 22:6).

For instance, if the parents are drinking, smoking, cheating, abusing each other, downing each other by speaking negatively towards each other, doing drugs, stealing, and tearing each other down etc... Then most likely the child or children can and will feel as though that is how it is supposed to be in the home and a relationship. This is why I wanted to talk about this little girl named Cmo. The beatings began at home and caused her to experience forty-four years of living an up-set life.

Chapter 19

Cmo Finds Her Biological Father

Cmo always felt a part of her was missing, like a void was in her life but she didn't know why. She often thought it was because Augustine failed to be a loving parent. But Douglas would always tell Cmo that he loved her, he never raised his hand towards her, and he would comfort her whenever he was around to do so. Augustine very rarely whooped Cmo if Douglas was around because he would always take up for her, whether she was right or wrong. Now older with children of her own, Cmo would sit and think about how her children's fathers had the opportunity to be great fathers but they failed to do so.

She had always felt a connection with Douglas because she and him were alike in so many ways, but in the back of her mind remained the question "Who is my biological father?" Augustine never told her, in fact, if Cmo ever asked, Augustine would get this awkward look in her eyes.

She would begin to tear up and then a wave of rage would sweep over her like a forest consumed with fire. She would, then, whoop Cmo, as if Cmo stole her last breath. Those would be the worst beatings she'd get so she became terrified to ask. But now that she was old enough to find out on her own, she didn't tell Augustine about her devised plan to seek out her biological father.

One day, as she was over to her grandmother's house, she began to ask her who she thought her father was. Her grandmother was shocked to be asked such a question. It had completely slipped her mind that Cmo was Pamela's child. But her grandmother felt it best to have Cmo ask her mother that question because the subject was uncharted territory, and in order to reveal that secret, an explanation would have to be involved. But Cmo was traumatized since childhood, so she didn't want to ask Augustine because she knew that it would upset her. The next best source would have been Pamela, but Cmo never mentioned these things to her before, so she didn't know how Pamela would react.

One day Cmo got the strength enough to call Pamela, she was nervous, but Cmo knew that if she ever wanted the truth then it would have to come straight from the horse's (Pamela) mouth. Cmo hung up three times before she actually opened her mouth to speak to Pamela, but she could hear the frustration in her voice when she answered.

PAMELA: "Hello, hello who the hell is this playing on my phone?!"

CMO: "Hi Pam, it's Cmo"

PAMELA: "Cmo? Cmo baby is that you? To what do I owe this pleasant surprise?"

CMO: "Yes it's me; I just wanted to call to ask you a question"

Cmo was very hesitant because she knew that it was a touchy subject, but her heart yearned to find out the truth. The only thing that worried her was the fear of the answer bringing back painful memories for Pamela. She didn't know the full story; was Pam raped, was she beaten? Cmo said a silent prayer, took a deep breath, and asked....

CMO: "Pam I know you are my biological mother, I have known this from a very young age. But what I don't know is... who's my father?"

Pamela sat in silence listening to Cmo as she went on...

CMO: "Every time I asked my mother, she would get so upset and she would beat me, it had gotten so bad that I just stopped asking. But I deserve to know who he is; I need to know who I am and I can't find out who I am with such a big part of me is missing."

There was complete silence on the phone but Cmo knew that Pam was still on the other end. Cmo couldn't help but feel guilty; she had opened up stored memories. Then she heard Pam's muffled cries, and she instantly withdrew her question.

CMO: "Pam I'm sorry, don't worry about it…"

PAMELA: "No Cmo baby I want you to know, you deserve to know but I just don't know how to tell you."

CMO: "Pam this would close such a big chapter in my life, but if it is too painful of a memory for you then please don't worry about it."

PAMELA: "Cmo, Douglas is your father, your biological father. He and I had an affair and you were the product of our deceit. I am so sorry you had to find out like this but it's the truth."

Cmo couldn't believe what her ears had just heard. Douglas, the only man she ever knew as her father, was her actual father. All her life she felt a special connection with him, and she thought it was because he was a loving parent, but in all actuality, she was his biological daughter. That is why they looked so much alike, same eyes, nose, face shape, and slender physique.

Then she thought about Augustine, having to look into her face and be reminded [everyday] of the deception from her husband and her sister, that is when she cried. She now understood the motive behind Augustine's rage; it was because Cmo was the product of betrayal. To have your husband cheat on you with your sister, and then she ends up getting pregnant. Now there is a living breathing thing to remind you, daily, of their disloyalty. Then you try desperately to get rid of the family's shame, only to have it survive and be thrust upon you like an infectious disease. Cmo was her mother's unwanted child because she was the product of infidelity, her father's infidelity.

***

Cmo didn't want Augustine to know that she knew who her real father was, but Pamela ended up telling Augustine about the entire conversation she had with Cmo. Though Augustine was upset, she wasn't upset with the fact that Cmo knew, but she wanted to be the one to tell her. Augustine had already made up in her mind that she was going to tell Cmo the truth, but she wanted to do it with a deep explanation followed by an apology.

She ended up telling Cmo that she had a difficult time forgiving her father's betrayal because the memory was still there, and she saw it in Cmo. She knew she was wrong, but her anger was stronger than her judgment, and it continued to grow and fester every time she looked into Cmo's eyes. But the sin wasn't in Cmo, the sin was in the act and she had finally realized this, but by then it was too late. She apologized to Cmo, not only for allowing her anger to destroy Cmo's innocence, but also for not loving her how a mother should. Though Cmo was a mother and grandmother, Augustine vowed to spend the rest of her life showing Cmo that love that she yearned for since she was child; pure motherly love.

Chapter 20

Augustine's Love

Augustine became Cmo's greatest companion in supporting love. When Cmo lost her youngest daughter, and found out who her biological father was, a relationship happened between her and Augustine. They began going to church and in doing so, their relationship flourished; the two were unstoppable. Love became the new driving force for the both of them.

They both begin to love and appreciate one another. Cmo actually moved back home (into her mother's home at age 44) and it was just her and her mother for 3 months. That was 3 months of quality time, communication, and getting to know each other. At forty-four years of age, Cmo and Augustine began speaking to each other like mother and daughter should; in the tones of I love you, I appreciate you, and you are my friend.

They were able to bury the past abuses and neglects. Until one day they were have a loving conversation; the dialogue was so sweet, and then Augustine began calling Cmo, 'Precious.' Precious actually began feeling better about herself, she started standing tall, she began to figure out that her mother could love and that love was so real and genuine. Cmo began to feel important, and her whole mindset changed. She was loved, she was not dumb, she was not stupid, she was good for something, she was going to be something, and she will be somebody.

Now Cmo has become 'Precious' to her mother. Cmo's happiness with her mother was all she ever wanted and she knew that nothing would ever come between that. Cmo began to feel life in her body once again. She needed to find a means to help others who were misunderstood and wanted a way out of the abusive nature they were in. Augustine suggested for Cmo to begin a business in regards to helping others as she has for years. Cmo felt that it was something she needed to do to show her heart and the love she had for her deceased children. Now with the understandings of self-respect, self-love, self-appreciation, self-reliance, self-worth, self-rebuke, and communication between each other, Cmo found love for her mother and for herself.

Cmo became so busy trying to prove her mother wrong in her rearing, that she became the abuser of them both. But her mother never gave up, because she knew of a God who would prevail; and he did. Augustine prayers had come true. She would often pray for understanding, peace, and for the covering of her child who was lost. She would plead for her child's safety to God; continuously, never failing to please her God. She would only work the motherhood in the manner in which she knew how while praying for guidance.

She wanted something different for her children and saw its future in her daughter Cmo. She knew Cmo would be a change for her life and this was her way of pushing Cmo into her purpose. She never wanted to hurt her child; she loved ALL of her children, but never understood the meaning of the love as a mother because she, herself, never understood her mother's love. But her daughter, Cmo, came through just as she predicted years ago. Cmo learned "LOVE".

Chapter 21

"LOVE" Learning Our Value Everyday

With these two; they were too busy trying to change each other, when the change needed to come from within. This is with the understanding that children will mimic their environment. In Augustine's life she knew abuse; Cmo saw the pain in her mother and Cmo lived her pain, her mother's pain, and the pain of others through abuse and violence.

However, Cmo refused to become a victim but in her ability of not understanding the illness of abuse and violence, she fell into abuse and violence; and when she fell, she fell hard. Cmo fell into an unconscious state of "self-destruction". Cmo became "STORM" a person of anger and deceit; Augustine became a woman of God, who prayed without cease, who had truly found love. In any relationship there are no winners or losers, there is only compromise and love. And love begins in you.

Always allow for freedom of speech; with respect. This will allow the home moral and behavioral development. This will also, enable each person to think and not judge or look at the next person in a negative way. Stop looking at others in a manner of judgment. Look at self and become your own critic. What does your mirror tell you? Become familiar with yourself, you may have some of the same tendency of the person for which you are in judgment of. By taking the blinders off, you will begin to focus on your inner person. Define self and "LOVE" self-daily; because when one learns their value, they will understand that their worth is "Love".

Who is "Cmo"? Cmo is the reflection of self, Cmo could be you. There is a little of Cmo in each of us; Cmo is the person within. Through Cmo's eyes the world presented darkness but her soul has been renewed and the light of "LOVE" shines through. She now knows who she is and her purpose in life, she is worth loving. In short Cmo is defined as SEE MORE.

Now to say "I want to be just like you" is a statement that warrants great consideration. Be careful of these words because to see a person's accomplishments provide a vain understanding to see their struggles is reality. You are asking for all the pains and hardships of the person in question. Do you really want to be like Cmo? No, no you don't! Be you, and love who you are, inside and out. Never covet a person's life, thinking that they have it better and easier than you. Live up to your own standards. You are not me. You are you. And, you are amazing just for being who you are.

~To All I give Love and to Love I give my All~

You Are Loved

The Author's Prayer

Lord Jesus I pray this book destroys the strongholds that causes us to be subjected to pain and disappointments. I pray that God in Heaven hear our cry and deliver us from the vulnerable spirit of our lack of feeling love and teach us how to begin to apply "LOVE'Learning Our Value Everyday'" to our lives. I pray we understand that "God in Heaven" the creator of all, loves us. We must keep a prayer connection with the Father in Heaven. With prayer we understand according to scripture 1 Corinthians 10:13 13 "There hath no temptation taken hold of you but such as is common to man. But God is faithful; He will not suffer you to be tempted beyond that which ye are able to bear, but with the temptation will also make a way to escape, that ye may be able to bear it." With prayer we understand according to the scripture Isaiah 43:19-21 "See, I am doing a new thing! Now it springs up; do you not perceive it I am making a way in the wilderness and streams in the wasteland. The wild animals honor me, the jackals and the owls, because I provide water in the wilderness and streams in the wasteland, to give drink to my people, my chosen, the people I formed for myself that they may proclaim my praise. He is my provider." With prayer we understand according to scripture Philippians 4:19 "But my God shall supply all your need according to his (God) riches in glory by Christ Jesus." Now, say unto you, "I believe upon these things in Jesus name and I am blessed in God".

Amen

www.ingramcontent.com/pod-product-compliance
Lightning Source LLC
Chambersburg PA
CBHW070640160426
43194CB00009B/1525